5&1 DIET cookbook

200 TASTY RECIPES TO HELP YOU REGAIN YOUR IDEAL SHAPE WITHOUT STRESS WHILE KEEPING YOU HEALTHY AND SUPER ENERGETIC

Annalisa Williams

Copyright - 2021 -

All rights reserved.

The content contained within this book may not be reproduced, duplicated or transmitted without direct written permission from the author or the publisher.

Under no circumstances will any blame or legal responsibility be held against the publisher, or author, for any damages, reparation, or monetary loss due to the information contained within this book. Either directly or indirectly.

Legal Notice:

This book is copyright protected. This book is only for personal use. You cannot amend, distribute, sell, use, quote or paraphrase any part, or the content within this book, without the consent of the author or publisher.

Disclaimer Notice:

Please note the information contained within this document is for educational and entertainment purposes only. All effort has been executed to present accurate, up to date, and reliable, complete information. No warranties of any kind are declared or implied. Readers acknowledge that the author is not engaging in the rendering of legal, financial, medical or professional advice. The content within this book has been derived from various sources. Please consult a licensed professional before attempting any techniques outlined in this book.

By reading this document, the reader agrees that under no circumstances is the author responsible for any losses, direct or indirect, which are incurred as a result of the use of information contained within this document, including, but not limited to, - errors, omissions, or inaccuracies.

TABLE OF CONTENTS

Introduction — 10
Chapter 1
What 5&1 Diet Consist? — 12
Chapter 2
The benefit of 5&1 diet — 16
Chapter 3
Why is 5&1 diet so Effective in Losing Weight? — 20
Chapter 4
Why 5&1 diet Rather than other diet? — 24
Chapter 5
5&1 diet plans — 26
Chapter 6
How Easy is to Follow 5&1 diet — 30
Chapter 7
Food to eat and food to Avoid — 32

Chapter 8
Lean and Green Recipes — 36

Salmon Florentine — 37
- Tomato Braised Cauliflower with Chicken — 37
- Braised Collard Greens in Peanut Sauce with Pork Tenderloin — 38
- Tomatillo and Green Chili Pork Stew — 38
- Cloud Bread — 39
- Avocado Lime Shrimp Salad — 39
- Broccoli Cheddar Breakfast Bake — 40
- Grilled Mahi Mahi with Jicama Slaw — 40
- Rosemary Cauliflower Rolls — 41
- Mediterranean Chicken Salad — 41

Chapter 9
Fueling Recipes — 42
- Fueling Mousse — 43
- Baked Cheesy Eggplant — 43

- Tabasco Anzac — 44
- Sweet Potato Casserole — 44
- Easter Bunny — 45
- High Protein Chipotle Cheddar Quesadilla — 46
- Zucchini Boats with Beef and Pimiento Rojo — 46
- Avocado Shrimp Cucumber Bites — 47
- Crispy Cauliflowers — 47
- Strawberry-Avocado Toast with Balsamic Glaze — 48

Chapter 10.
Fueling recipes 2 — 50
- Tropical Greens Smoothie — 51
- Vitamin C Smoothie Cubes — 51
- Overnight Chocolate Chia Pudding — 52
- Slow Cooker Savory Butternut Squash Oatmeal — 52
- Carrot Cake Oatmeal — 53
- Spiced Sorghum and Berries — 53
- Raw-Cinnamon-Apple Nut Bowl — 54
- Peanut Butter and Cacao Breakfast Quinoa — 54
- Vanilla Buckwheat Porridge — 55
- Polenta with Seared Pears — 55
- Best Whole Wheat Pancakes — 56
- Spiced Pumpkin Muffins — 56

Chapter 11.
Breakfast — 58
- Pizza Hack — 59
- Sweet Cashew Cheese Spread — 59
- Mini Zucchini Bites — 60
- Whole-Wheat Blueberry Muffins — 60
- Walnut Crunch Banana Bread — 61
- Plant-Powered Pancakes — 61
- Shake Cake Fueling — 62
- Biscuit Pizza — 62
- Mini Mac in a Bowl — 63
- Lean and Green Smoothie 1 — 63
- Lean and Green Smoothie 2 — 64
- Lean and Green Chicken Pesto Pasta — 64
- Mini Mac in a Bowl — 65
- Lean and Green Smoothie 1 — 65
- Lean and Green Smoothie 2 — 66
- Lean and Green Chicken Pesto Pasta — 66

Chapter 12.
Breakfast 2 — 68

- Alkaline Blueberry Spelt Pancakes — 69
- Alkaline Blueberry Muffins — 69
- Crunchy Quinoa Meal — 70
- Coconut Pancakes — 70
- Quinoa Porridge — 71
- Amaranth Porridge — 71
- Banana Barley Porridge — 72
- Zucchini Muffins — 72
- Millet Porridge — 73
- Jackfruit Vegetable Fry — 73
- Zucchini Pancakes — 74
- Squash Hash — 74
- Hemp Seed Porridge — 75
- Pumpkin Spice Quinoa — 75

CHAPTER 13

MAINS — 76

- Baked Ricotta with Pears — 77
- Pesto Zucchini Noodles — 78
- Stewed Herbed Fruit — 78
- Herbed Wild Rice — 79
- Buffalo Chicken Sliders — 79
- High Protein Chicken Meatballs — 80
- Barley Risotto — 80
- Risotto with Green Beans, Sweet Potatoes, and Peas — 81
- Maple Lemon Tempeh Cubes — 81
- Bok Choy with Tofu Stir Fry — 82
- Three-Bean Medley — 82
- Herbed Garlic Black Beans — 83
- Quinoa with Vegetables — 83

CHAPTER 14.

MAINS 2 — 84

- Balsamic Beef and Mushrooms Mix — 85
- Oregano Pork Mix — 85
- Simple Beef Roast — 86
- Chicken Breast Soup — 86
- Cauliflower Curry — 87
- Pork and Peppers Chili — 87
- Greek Style Quesadillas — 88
- Light Paprika Moussaka — 88
- Cucumber Bowl with Spices and Greek Yogurt — 89
- Stuffed Bell Peppers with Quinoa — 89
- Mediterranean Burrito — 90

- Sweet Potato Bacon Mash — 90
- Prosciutto Wrapped Mozzarella Balls — 91
- Garlic Chicken Balls — 91

Chapter 15.
Snacks recipes — 92
- Veggie Fritters — 93
- White Bean Dip — 93
- Eggplant Dip — 94
- Bulgur Lamb Meatballs — 94
- Cucumber Bites — 95
- Stuffed Avocado — 95
- Hummus with Ground Lamb — 96
- Wrapped Plums — 96
- Cucumber Sandwich Bites — 97
- Cucumber Rolls — 97
- Olives and Cheese Stuffed Tomatoes — 98
- Tomato Salsa — 98
- Chili Mango and Watermelon Salsa — 99
- Creamy Spinach and Shallots Dip — 99
- Feta Artichoke Dip — 100
- Avocado Dip — 100
- Goat Cheese and Chives Spread — 101

Chapter 16.
Snack recipes 2 — 102
- Bacon Cheeseburger — 103
- Cheeseburger Pie — 103
- Personal Pizza Biscuit — 104
- Chicken and Mushrooms — 104
- Chicken Enchilada Bake — 105
- Mediterranean Chicken Salad — 105
- Jalapeno Lentil (Chickpea) Burgers + Avocado Mango Pico — 106
- Grandma's Rice — 107
- Baked Beef Zucchini — 107
- Baked Tuna with Asparagus — 108
- Lamb Stuffed Avocado — 108

Chapter 17.
Vegetables — 110
- Green Beans — 111
- Asparagus Avocado Soup — 111
- Sweet Potato Chips — 112

- Fried Zucchini · 112
- Fried Avocado · 113
- Vegetables in air Fryer · 113
- Crispy Rye Bread Snacks with Guacamole and Anchovies · 114
- Mushrooms Stuffed with Tomato · 114
- Fennel and Arugula Salad With Fig Vinaigrette · 115
- Mixed Potato Gratin · 115
- Green Pea Guacamole · 116

Chapter 18.
Vegetables 2 — 118

- Cauliflower Crust Pizza · 119
- Thai Roasted Veggies · 119
- Roasted Squash Puree · 120
- Creamy Spinach and Mushroom Lasagna · 120
- Kale Slaw and Strawberry Salad + Poppyseed Dressing · 121
- Roasted Root Vegetables · 121
- Hummus · 122
- Crispy-Topped Baked Vegetables · 122
- Vegan Edamame Quinoa Collard Wraps · 123
- Grilled Eggplants · 123

Chapter 19.
Meat — 124

- Tomatillo and Green Chili Pork Stew · 125
- Tomato Braised Cauliflower with Chicken · 125
- Grilled Chicken Power Bowl With Green Goddess Dressing · 126
- Cumin-Lime Steak · 126
- Chicken Strips · 127
- Chicken Stir Fry · 127
- Turkey Taco · 128
- Braised Collard Greens In Peanut Sauce With Pork Tenderloin · 128
- Turkey Caprese Meatloaf Cups · 129
- Mediterranean Grilled Chicken · 129
- Avocado Chicken Salad · 130
- Chicken Crust Margherita Pizza · 130

Chapter 20.
Soups and stews — 132

- Roasted Tomato Soup · 133
- Cheeseburger Soup · 133
- Quick Lentil Chili · 134

- Lemon Garlic Oregano Chicken with Asparagus — 134
- Creamy Cauliflower Soup — 135
- Crackpot Chicken Taco Soup — 135
- Tofu Stir Fry With Asparagus — 136
- Cream of Thyme Tomato Soup — 136
- Mushroom & Jalapeño Stew — 137
- Easy Cauliflower Soup — 137
- Cauliflower Soup — 138
- Lime-Mint Soup — 138
- Savory Split Pea Soup — 139

CHAPTER 21.
SMOOTHIES — 140

- Avocado Blueberry Smoothie — 141
- Vegan Blueberry Smoothie — 141
- Berry Peach Smoothie — 142
- Cantaloupe Blackberry Smoothie — 142
- Cantaloupe Kale Smoothie — 143
- Mix Berry Cantaloupe Smoothie — 143
- Avocado Kale Smoothie — 144
- Apple Kale Cucumber Smoothie — 144
- Refreshing Cucumber Smoothie — 145
- Cauliflower Veggie Smoothie — 145
- Soursop Smoothie — 146
- Cucumber-Ginger Water — 146
- Strawberry Milkshake — 147
- Cactus Smoothie — 147
- Prickly Pear Juice — 148
- Cucumber-Ginger Water — 148

CHAPTER 22.
DESSERTS — 150

- Asparagus Green Scramble — 151
- No Bake Fueling Peanut Butter Brownies — 151
- Peanut Butter Brownie Ice Cream Sandwiches — 152
- Cranberry Salad — 152
- Chicken Salad With Pineapple And Pecans — 153
- Zucchini Fritter — 153
- Healthy Broccoli Salad — 154
- Biscuit Pizza — 154
- Granola — 155
- Delicious Zucchini Quiche — 155
- Cobb Salad with Blue Cheese Dressing — 156
- Vanilla Bean Frappuccino — 156

Dark Chocolate Mochaccino Ice Bombs	157
Chocolate Bark With Almonds	157

CHAPTER 23.
DESSERTS   158

Chocolate Bars	159
Blueberry Muffins	159
Chia Pudding	160
Avocado Pudding	160
Delicious Brownie Bites	161
Pumpkin Balls	161
Smooth Peanut Butter Cream	162
Vanilla Avocado Popsicles	162
Chocolate Popsicle	163
Raspberry Ice Cream	163
Chocolate Frosty	164
Chocolate Almond Butter Brownie	164
Peanut Butter Fudge	165
Almond Butter Fudge	165
CONCLUSION	**166**

INTRODUCTION

The 5&1 Diet has been subjected to various studies to prove its efficacy in weight loss. Different studies were published in various journals indicating that those who follow this program are able to see significant changes in as little as 8 weeks and that people can achieve their long-term health goals with the 5&1 Diet.

While the initial 5&1 ideal weight plan is quite restrictive, maintenance phases 3&3 allow for greater variety of less processed foods and snacks, which can facilitate weight loss.

Under this diet regimen, dieters are required to follow a weight plan that includes five fueling a day and one lean green meal daily. However, there are also other regimens of the 5&1 Diet if the five fuels a day is too much for you. And since this is a commercial diet, you have access to 5&1 coaches and become part of a community that will encourage you to succeed in your weight loss journey. Moreover, this diet is also designed for people who want to transition from their old habits to healthier ones.

The diet is a set of three programs, two of which focus on weight loss and one that is best for weight maintenance, if you are not trying to lose weight. The plans are high in protein and low in carbohydrates and calories to stimulate weight loss. Each program requires you to eat at least half of the food in the form of numerous 5&1 healthy prepackaged foods.

Since the plan requires the intake of carbohydrates, protein and fat, it is also a relatively balanced plan when it comes to food groups.

When it comes to weight loss, experts say that while 5&1 can help because it is essentially less caloric, it is unlikely to improve your eating habits permanently. You are more likely to gain weight after stopping the diet.

Also, diet experts warn that this pattern may not contain enough calories to meet your body's needs. "In terms of overall health and nutrition, as well as convenience, this diet isn't at the top of my list of best approaches." she says.

If you are interested in trying this, consider working with an experienced registered dietitian who can help you stay properly fed as you strive to achieve your desired weight.

For the most desirable 5 and 1 weight plan, eat 5 foods per day, plus a low carb lean meal and a low carb elective snack.

Although Initial Plan 5 & 1 is reasonably restrictive, Protection Segment 3 & 3 allows for a greater variety of less processed foods and snacks, which can also make weight loss easier and more persistent for long period

The bottom line is, that the 5&1 weight loss plan promotes weight loss via low calorie prepackaged meals; low carb homemade food, and personalized coaching; at the same time, as this system promotes quick-time period weight and fat loss, similarly research is wanted to assess whether it encourages the everlasting way of life adjustments needed for long-time period achievement.

CHAPTER 1
WHAT 5&1 DIET CONSIST?

How It Works

The 5&1 diet is a practice that aims to reduce or maintain current weight. It is a diet that recommends eating a combination of processed foods called fuels and home-cooked meals (lean and green meals). It is believed that it sticks to the brand product (input) and supplements it with meat, vegetables, and fatty snacks; this will keep you satisfied and nourished. At the same you don't need to worry much about losing muscles because you are eating enough protein and consuming too few calories. And that way, the individual who practices the diet can lose around 12 pounds in just 12 weeks using the ideal 5&1 weight plan.

In short, this diet is a program that focuses on cutting calories and reducing carbohydrates in meals. To do this effectively, combine packaged foods called fuels with home-cooked meals, which encourages weight loss.

Like many commercial plans, 5&1 involves buying most of the foods permitted on a diet in packaged form. The company deals on a wide range of food products that they call "fuels"—on its website. These include pancakes, shakes, pasta dishes, soups, cookies, mashed potatoes, and popcorn.

Users pick the plan that best suits them. The 5 & 1 plan entails eating five small meals per day. The meals can be selected from more than 60 substitutable fuels, including one "lean and green" meal, probably veggies or protein that you will prepare by yourself. The Optimal Essential Kit, costing $356.15, provides 119 servings, or about 20 days' worth.

A flexible option is the 4 & 2 & 1 plan. It just contains four supplies a day; you can choose and create two of your "lean and green" meals and one of the snacks purchased from 5&1. Plus, with a similar mix of prepared foods, a 140-serving kit costs $ 399.00 Is

How Much Does 5&1 Cost?

In comparison, the United States Department of Agriculture estimates that a woman whose ages range from 10-50 can follow a nutritious diet while spending as little as $166.40 per month on groceries. As long as she is preparing all her meals at home.

How Nutritious Is 5&1 Diet?

Below is the breakdown comparison of meals' nutritional content on the Weight 5&1 Plan and the federal government's 2015 Dietary Guidelines for Americans.

	Weight 5&1 Plan	Federal Government Recommendation
Calories	800-1,000	Men 19-25: 2,800 26-45: 2,600 46-65: 2,400 65+: 2,200 Women 19-25: 2,200 26-50: 2,000 51+: 1,800
Total fat % of Calorie Intake	20%	20%-35%
Total Carbohydrates % of Calorie Intake	40%	45%-65%
Sugars	10%-20%	N/A
Fiber	25 g – 30 g	Men 19-30: 34 g. 31-50: 31 g. 51+: 28 g. Women 19-30: 28 g. 31-50: 25 g. 51+: 22 g.
Protein	40%	10%-35%

Sodium	Under 2,300 mg	Under 2,300 mg.
Potassium	Average 3,000 mg	At least 4,700 mg.
Calcium	1,000 mg – 1,200 mg	Men 1,000 mg. Women 19-50: 1,000 mg. 51+: 1,200 mg.

CHAPTER 2
THE BENEFIT OF 5&1 DIET

5&1's program may be a solid match for you on the off chance that you need a diet plan that is clear and simple to follow, that will assist you with getting in shape rapidly, and offers worked in social help.

When embarking on any new diet regimen, you may experience some difficulties along the way. Below are the reasons why this diet regimen is considered as the easiest to follow among all commercial diet regimens.

<u>Accomplishes Rapid Weight Loss</u>

Most solid individuals require around 1600 to 3000 calories for each day to keep up their weight. Limiting that number to as low as 800 basically ensures weight loss for a great many people.

5&1 Plan is intended for brisk weight loss, making it a strong choice for somebody with a clinical motivation to shed pounds quick.

You enter the fat-loss stage in just 3 days. Look for Weight loss story on YouTube to see how many people out there are losing an impressing amount of weight, even 20 or more pounds in a week.

The average of 12 pounds in 12 weeks on the website counts all the people that do it by themselves, and nobody knows how many times they actually follow the plan, how many times they cheat, how much water they drink, exercise, etc.

<u>Easy to Follow</u>

As the diet depend on generally a prepackaged   Fuels, you are only accountable for doing one meal a day on the 5&1 Plan.

Although you are encouraged to prepare 1 to 3 green and lean foods a day, depending on your strategy, they are very simple to prepare, as the program will include detailed recipes and a list of food options to choose from.

Also, those who don't like to cook can purchase packaged meals called Flavors of Home to replace Lean and Green meals.

Bundled Items Offer Comfort

5&1's shakes, soups, and all other feast substitution items are conveyed legitimately to your entryway—a degree of comfort that numerous different diets don't offer.

In spite of the fact that you should search for your own elements for "lean and green" dinners, the home conveyance choice for 5&1's "Fuels" spares time and vitality.

When the items show up, they're anything but difficult to get ready and make phenomenal snatch and go suppers.

Packaged Products

They will be delivered directly at home, and they are quick-to-make and grab-and-go.

Social Support and Coaching

Stay motivated, do not cheat. Point out how people on coaching achieve a much faster and more massive weight loss.

Offers Social Help

Social help is a crucial part of achievement with any weight loss plan. 5&1's training project and gathering can give worked in consolation and backing for clients.

5&1's health coaches are available throughout the weight loss and maintenance programs.

Eliminates the Guesswork

You don't have to worry about what to eat all day, just cook it once a day or every other day.

Some people find that the hardest part of the diet is the psychological effort required to understand what to eat every day, or even every dinner.

5&1 reduces the pressure of party planning and "running out of options" by offering customers set foods with "supplies" and rules for "simple and green" meals.

It's Not a Ketogenic Diet

Carbs are allowed and higher than the majority of weight-loss diets out there, just not the refined ones.

No Counting Calories

You don't really need to count your calories when following this type of diet, just as long as you stick with the rule of Fuels, meals, snacks and water intake depending on your preference may it be 5&1, 4&2&1 or 3&3.

CHAPTER 3
WHY IS 5&1 DIET SO EFFECTIVE IN LOSING WEIGHT?

Most "supplies" contain between 100 and 110 calories each, which means you can consume around 1000 calories a day on this diet. As a result of this approach, the US News and World Report ranked it second on its list of the best diets for fast weight loss, but 32nd on its list of the best diets for healthy eating. London recognizes that there are other ways to lasting weight loss: "Eat meals and snacks that incorporate lots of products, seeds, nuts, greens, 100% whole grains, eggs, seafood, poultry, greens, low-fat dairy products. Fat, lean meat plus a little indulgence is the best way to lose weight sustainably in the long run. " So will the 5&1 diet help you lose weight?

The amount of weight you lose after following the OPTAVIA diet programs depends on factors such as your starting weight, as well as your activity and loyalty to following the plan. OPTAVIA, launched in 2017, represents the Nutryfast lifestyle brand and the coaching community. Previous studies have been done using Nutrifast products, not the new 5&1 products. Although the 5&1 products represent a new line, Nutrifast reported to US News that they have an identical macronutrient profile, making them interchangeable With Nutryfast products. Consequently, we believe that the following studies are applicable in the evaluation of this diet. Little specific research has been published on the 5&1 brand. The studies, like most diets, were small, with numerous dropouts. Research seems to confirm this. On the other hand, the long-term expectation is less promising

Here's a more detailed look at the data:

According to a 2017 Nutryfast-sponsored study, more than 70% of overweight adults who received individual behavioral support and underwent Nutryfast have lost more than 5% of their body weight since their last visit, which is four to 24 weeks. then.

According to a 2016 study published in the journal Obesity and with partial support from Nutryfast, obese adults lost 8.8% of their body weight after 12 weeks with 5&1 style training and Nutryfast products, and also 12, 1% of your body weight if you were taking Phentermine at the same time, which is a weight loss drug that can reduce binge eating.

However, the researchers found only one long-term study, which indicated no benefit for these 12-month plans. The researchers found that there is also an increased risk of complications, such as gallstones, on ultra-low-calorie programs.

However, the study found that the effect was reduced beyond six months of reporting the results.

During a small study, designed and funded by Nutryfast and published in 2010 in the Nutrition Journal, 90 obese adults were randomly assigned to either the low-calorie diet or the 5 & 1 plan according to government guidelines. The Nutryfast dieters, however, regained more than 4.5 kg 24 weeks later, after the calories gradually increased. The others gained only 2 pounds. Compared to the initial exercise, the Nutryfast group had more muscle mass and less body fat at week 40, but it did not outperform the control group. Eventually, about half of the Nutryfast group and more than half of the control group withdrew.

According to a Nutryfast-funded study of 119 overweight or obese type 2 diabetics published in Diabetes Educator in 2008, dieters were randomly assigned to either a Nutryfast diabetes plan or a diet based on the recommendations of the American Association of Diabetes.

After 34 weeks, the Nutryfast group had lost an average of 4.5 kilos, but had regained almost 1.5 kilos after 86 weeks. Over 34 weeks, those who followed the ADA-based diet lost an average of 3 pounds; they got everything back plus an extra pound in 86 weeks. By the end of the year, about 80% had given up

According to an analysis funded by Nutryfast and published in 2008 in the journal Eating and Weight Disorders, researchers analyzed the medical records of 324 people who were on a diet who were overweight or obese and who were also taking a prescription appetite suppressant. In 12 weeks, they lost an average of 21 pounds, in 24 weeks they weighed 26 1/2 pounds, and 27 pounds in 52 weeks.

Furthermore, for approximately 80% of them, at least 5% of the initial weight had been lost in all three evaluations. This is great if you are obese, because losing just 5-10% of your current weight can help prevent some diseases.

However, these numbers are accompanied by some asterisks. First, because they are based on people who completed or completed the 52-week program, they were more likely to lose weight. (Weight loss was still effective, but less pronounced in a cessation analysis.)

Second, a review of patient data is given less importance than a study with a control group. Finally, in a survey in which researchers divided dieters into consumer groups on Nutryfast, that is, those who recognized that they consume at least two shakes a day at each check-in and those who are inconsistent, it is say, the rest. , weight loss was not significantly different

In a 2013 study in the International Journal of Obesity that looked at 120 men and women ages 19 to 65, half of whom were using Nutryfast, while the other half were limited to cutting calories, researchers found that those who on the Nutryfast diet lost an average of 16 1/2 pounds after 26 weeks, compared to the control group, who lost 4 kg.

The 5&1 diet has generated headlines throughout the year. Users must enroll in a low-calorie meal plan and then purchase the packaged foods that are part of the chosen plan. In this sitemap, no food group is completely off limits, promising "permanent transformation, one healthy habit at a time."

Although it has many fans, 5&1 is not cheap. The US News and World Report ranked it second in the rapid weight loss category. In 2018, it was also a popular diet on Google. Famous "cake chef" Buddy Valastro credits 5&1 for his recent weight loss.

Do you want to try the 5&1 diet? Will this really help you lose weight? Here's everything for you: the health implications, if they are difficult to follow, and the likelihood of reaching your weight loss goal.

CHAPTER 4
WHY 5&1 DIET RATHER THAN OTHER DIET?

Calorie Restriction Impact

Despite the fact that 5&1's eating routine arrangement stresses eating every now and again for the duration of the day, every one of its "fuels" just gives 110 calories. "Lean and green" foods are additionally low in calories.

At the point when you're eating fewer calories all in all, you may discover the arrangement leaves you ravenous and unsatisfied. You may likewise feel all the more effectively exhausted and even crabby.

Weariness and Isolation at Mealtimes

5&1's dependence on meal substitutions can meddle with the social parts of getting ready and eating food.

Clients may think that it's clumsy or baffling to have a shake or bar at family supper time or when feasting out with companions.

How It Compares with others

The 5&1 Diet can be more viable for fast weight reduction than different plans basically in view of what a limited number of calories its fuels and "lean and green" meals give.

U.S. News and World Report positioned 5&1 as the number two best eating routine for quick weight reduction (attached with Atkins, keto, and Weight Watchers).1

The 2019 U.S. News and World Report Best Diets positioned the 5&1 Diet 31st in Best Diets Overall and gave it a general score of 2.7/5.

5&1 requires less "mental acrobatic" than contenders like Weight Watchers, (for which you need to gain proficiency with an arrangement of focuses) or keto (for which you should intently follow and evaluate macronutrients).

5&1's instructing segment is similar to Weight Watchers and Jenny Craig, the two of which urge members to select in for meetups to get social help.

The exceptionally handled nature of most nourishments you'll eat on the 5&1 diet can be a drawback contrasted with the variety of new, entire nourishments you can eat on increasingly independently directed plans, for example, Atkins.

Calorie restriction is essential to weight reduction and the 5&1 option is particularly conducive to shedding weight rapidly with an 800-one thousand calorie nutritional plan. Carbs also are stored low with a decent amount of protein per serving which is right for effective weight reduction in maximum instances.

Plus, carb and calorie restrict have shown to have many health advantages which includes advanced glucose metabolism, adjustments in frame composition, reduced danger of cardiovascular chance elements, and other disorder chance elements as nicely.

But the 5&1 may not be for anyone as dropping weight quickly and excessive calorie restrict can be damaging to your health and also you virtually won't experience excellent, at the same time as muscle loss is likewise an opportunity. 800-one thousand energy are quite low, in standard.

However, for weight loss, eating 800-1000 energy can be safe and effective if no longer applied for extended periods.

Research suggests that too few calories can have an effect on metabolism over the years that could make you to regain weight.

But this will additionally be due to long term habits as there are also several different variables to recall in terms of the differences among people. Weight loss isn't continually easy and retaining it off may be even more difficult however it requires everlasting life-style changes.

5&1 additionally recommends 30 minutes a day of exercise which is likewise important for maintaining weight off and maintaining proper health.

CHAPTER 5
5&1 DIET PLANS

The 5&1 Diet encourages people to limit the number of calories that they should take daily. Under this program, dieters are encouraged to consume between 800 and 1000 calories daily. For this to be possible, dieters are encouraged to opt for healthier food items as well as meal replacements. But unlike other types of commercial diet regimens, the 5&1 Diet comes in different variations. There are currently three variations of the 5&1 Diet Plan that one can choose from according to one's needs.

- 5&1 5&1 Diet Plan: This is the most common version of the 5&1 Diet, and it involves eating five prepackaged meals from the Optimal Health Fuels and one home-made balanced meal.

- 4&2&1 Octavia Diet Plan: This diet plan is designed for people who want to have flexibility while following this regimen. Under this program, dieters are encouraged to eat more calories and have more flexible food choices. This means that they can consume 4 prepackaged Optimal Health Fuels food, three home-cooked meals from the Lean and Green, and one snack daily.

- 5&2&2 5&1 Diet Plan: This diet plan is perfect for individuals who prefer to have a flexible meal plan in order to achieve a healthy weight. It is recommended for a wide variety of people. Under this diet regimen, dieters are required to eat 5 fuels, 2 lean and green meals, and 2 healthy snacks.

- 3&3 Diet Plan: This particular Diet Plan is created for people who have moderate weight problems and merely want to maintain a healthy body. Under this diet plan, dieters are encouraged to consume 3 Prepackaged Optimal Health Fuels and three home-cooked meals.

- 5&1 for Nursing Mothers: This diet regimen is designed for nursing mothers with babies of at least two months old. Aside from supporting breastfeeding mothers, it also encourages gradual weight loss.

- 5&1 for Diabetes: This Diet plan is designed for people who have Type 1 and Type 2 diabetes. The meal plans are designed so that dieters consume more green and lean meals, depending on their needs and condition.

- 5&1 for Gout: This diet regimen incorporates a balance of foods that are low in purines and moderate in protein.

- 5&1 for Seniors (65 years and older): Designed for seniors, this 5&1 Diet plan has some variations following the components of Fuels depending on the needs and activities of the senior dieters.

- 5&1 for Teen Boys and 5&1 for Teen Girls (13-18 years old): Designed for active teens, the 5&1 for Teens Boys and 5&1 for Teens Girls provide the right nutrition to growing teens.

- Regardless of which type of 5&1 Diet plan you choose, it is important that you talk with a coach to help you determine which plan is right for you based on your individual goals.

How to Start This Diet

The 5&1 Diet is comprised of different phases. A certified coach will educate you on the steps that you need to undertake if you want to follow this regimen., below are some the things you need to know, especially when you are still starting with this diet regimen.

Initial Steps

During this phase, people are encouraged to consume 800 to 1,000 calories to help you shed off at least 12 pounds within the next 12 weeks. For instance, if you are following the 5&1 Diet Plan, then you need to eat 1 meal every 2 or 3 hours and include a 30-minute moderate workout most days of your week. You need to consume not more than 100 grams of Carbs daily during this phase.

Further, consuming meals are highly encouraged. This phase also encourages the dieter to include 1 optional snack per day, such as ½ cup sugar-free gelatin, 3 celery sticks, and 12 ounces nuts. Aside from these things, below are other things that you need to remember when following this phase:

- Make sure that the portion size recommendations are for cooked weight and not the raw weight of your ingredients

- Opt for meals that are baked, grilled, broiled, or poached. Avoid frying foods, as this will increase your calorie intake.
- Eat at least 2 servings of fish rich in Omega-3 fatty acids. These include fishes like tuna, salmon, trout, mackerel, herring, and other cold-water fishes.
- Choose meatless alternatives like tofu and tempeh.
- Follow the program even when you are dining out. Keep in mind that drinking alcohol is discouraged when following this plan.

<u>Maintenance Phase</u>

As soon as you have attained your desired weight, the next phase is the transition stage. It is a 6-week stage that involves increasing your calorie intake to 1,550 per day. This is also the phase when you are allowed to add more varieties into your meal, such as whole grains, low-fat dairy, and fruits.

After six weeks, you can now move into the 3&3 Diet Plan, so you are required to eat three Lean and Green meals and 3 Fuels foods.

CHAPTER 6
HOW EASY IS TO FOLLOW 5&1 DIET

Practicing the 5&1 diet gives you an option of about 60 Fuels, but that is not to say you will still not have yearnings for other food options, especially those you are used to before taking up the diet plan.

All the recipes are readily available, and you can also take the option of dining out by following your guide. However, alcohol consumption is prohibited. You can order your meals easily or prepare them in your kitchen under a few minutes. You can easily get the needed tools to make your meals from your coach or request for help on the online community.

You can get various ideas for your lean and green meals by visiting the brand Pinterest page. You will also get a recipe conversion guide that you can use whenever you have trouble with your recipe measurement.

You might face many challenges whenever you decide to eat out. However, it is not impossible to eat out. To be on the safe side, the brand advised you to let your Lean and Green meals be the only option when you consider eating out. By going through the dining out guide, you will get the clue on how to navigate buffets, order beverages, and selecting condiments and toppings for your meals.

It is straightforward to choose a plan and make your order that will be delivered instantly. Food preparation is swift, and the only area where you can face difficulty is adding water and nuking in the microwave. Anyone with no knowledge of cooking can easily tackle and get over the preparation of preparing the meals without breaking a sweat.

The 5&1 coaches aim to help you adopt healthy habits. You will get weekly, and monthly support calls from the 5&1 coaches. Once you are a member of the community, you will also be able to partake in community events and have access to the nutrition support team, mainly composed of dietitians. Informational guides and FAQs can also be accessed online easily and for free.

The company says the recommended meals have a high "fullness index," which means that the high protein and fiber contents in the meals should help get full for an extended period.

The meals you will be taking are tailored for the weight and fat loss purpose and may not likely win a cuisine competition. It is pertinent to note that the 5&1 Fuels you will feed on will not contain flavors, artificial colors, or sweeteners.

No matter the plan you pick out, you start by using having a smartphone communique with a tutor to help determine which 5&1 plan to follow, set weight loss desires, and make yourself familiar with the application.

Eating out can be challenging, but still possible. If you love eating out, you can download 5&1's dining out guide. The guide comes with tips on how to navigate buffets, order beverages, and choose condiments. Aside from following the guide, you can also ask the chef to make substitutions for the ingredients used in cooking your food. For instance, you can ask the chef to serve no more than 7 ounces of steak and serve it with steamed broccoli instead of baked potatoes.

Opt for lean and green foods that have high fullness index. Eat foods that contain high protein and fiber content as they can keep you full for longer periods. In fact, many nutrition experts highlight the importance of satiety when it comes to weight loss.

You have access to knowledgeable coaches. If you follow the 5&1 Diet Plan, you have access to knowledgeable coaches and become a part of a community that will give you access to support calls and community events. You also have a standby nutrition support team that can answer your questions.

Irrespective of the diet plan you pick, you commence by having a teleconference with a certain coach to assist in determining which 5&1 diet plan to follow, established weight loss objectives, and acquaint yourself with the platform.

CHAPTER 7
FOOD TO EAT AND FOOD TO AVOID

There are a lot many foods that you can eat while following the 5&1 Diet. However, you must know these foods by heart. This is particularly true if you are just new to this diet, and you have to follow the 5&1 5&1 Diet Plan strictly. Thus, this section is dedicated to the types of foods that are recommended and those to avoid while following this diet regimen.

<u>Food to eat</u>

There are numerous categories of foods that can be eaten under this diet regimen. This section will break down the Lean and Green foods that you can eat while following this diet regime.

<u>Lean Foods</u>

Leanest Foods - These foods are considered to be the leanest as it has only up to 4 grams of total fat. Moreover, dieters should eat a 7-ounce cooked portion of these foods. Consume these foods with 1 healthy fat serving.

- Fish: Flounder, cod, haddock, grouper, Mahi, tilapia, tuna (yellowfin fresh or canned), and wild catfish.

- Shellfish: Scallops, lobster, crabs, shrimp

- Game meat: Elk, deer, buffalo

- Ground turkey or other meat: Should be 98% lean

- Meatless alternatives: 14 egg whites, 2 cups egg substitute, 5 ounces seitan, 1 ½ cups 1% cottage cheese, and 12 ounces non-fat 0% Greek yogurt

Leaner Foods - These foods contain 5 to 9 grams of total fat. Consume these foods with 1 healthy fat serving. Make sure to consume only 6 ounces of a cooked portion of these foods daily:

- Fish: Halibut, trout, and swordfish
- Chicken: White meat such as breasts as long as the skin is removed
- Turkey: Ground turkey as long as it is 95% to 97% lean.
- Meatless options: 2 whole eggs plus 4 egg whites, 2 whole eggs plus one cup egg substitute, 1 ½ cups 2% cottage cheese, and 12 ounces low fat 2% plain Greek yogurt

Lean Foods - These are foods that contain 10g to 20g total fat. When consuming these foods, there should be no serving of healthy fat. These include the following:

- Fish: Tuna (bluefin steak), salmon, herring, farmed catfish, and mackerel
- Lean beef: Ground, steak, and roast
- Lamb: All cuts
- Pork: Pork chops, pork tenderloin, and all parts. Make sure to remove the skin
- Ground turkey and other meats: 85% to 94% lean
- Chicken: Any dark meat
- Meatless options: 15 ounces extra-firm tofu, 3 whole eggs (up to two times per week), 4 ounces reduced-fat skim cheese, 8 ounces part-skim ricotta cheese, and 5 ounces tempeh

Healthy Fat Servings - Healthy fat servings are allowed under this diet. They should contain 5 grams of fat and less than grams of carbohydrates. Regardless of what type of Optavia Diet plan you follow, make sure that you add between 0 and 2 healthy fat servings daily. Below are the different healthy fat servings that you can eat:

- 1 teaspoon oil (any kind of oil)
- 1 tablespoon low carbohydrate salad dressing
- 2 tablespoons reduced-fat salad dressing
- 5 to 10 black or green olives
- 1 ½ ounce avocado
- 1/3-ounce plain nuts including peanuts, almonds, pistachios
- 1 tablespoon plain seeds such as chia, sesame, flax, and pumpkin seeds
- ½ tablespoon regular butter, mayonnaise, and margarine

Green Foods

This section will discuss the green servings that you still need to consume while following the 5&1 Diet Plan. These include all kinds of vegetables that have been categorized from lower, moderate, and high in terms of carbohydrate content. One serving of vegetables should be at ½ cup unless otherwise specified.

Lower Carbohydrate - These are vegetables that contain low amounts of carbohydrates. If you are following the 5&1 5&1 Diet Plan, then these vegetables are good for you.

- A cup of green leafy vegetables, such as collard greens (raw), lettuce (green leaf, iceberg, butterhead, and romaine), spinach (raw), mustard greens, spring mix, bok choy (raw), and watercress.

- ½ cup of vegetables including cucumbers, celery, radishes, white mushroom, sprouts (mung bean, alfalfa), arugula, turnip greens, escarole, nopales, Swiss chard (raw), jalapeno, and bok choy (cooked).

Moderate Carbohydrate - These are vegetables that contain moderate amounts of carbohydrates. Below are the types of vegetables that can be consumed in moderation:

- ½ cup of any of the following vegetables such as asparagus, cauliflower, fennel bulb, eggplant, Portabella mushrooms, kale, cooked spinach, summer squash (zucchini and scallop).

Higher Carbohydrates - Foods that are under this category contain a high amount of starch. Make sure to consume limited amounts of these vegetables.

- ½ cup of the following vegetables like chayote squash, red cabbage, broccoli, cooked collard and mustard greens, green or wax beans, kohlrabi, kabocha squash, cooked leeks, any peppers, okra, raw scallion, summer squash such as straight neck and crookneck, tomatoes, spaghetti squash, turnips, jicama, cooked Swiss chard, and hearts of palm.

Food to avoid

With the exclusion of carbohydrates in the prepackaged 5&1 Fuels, most carbohydrate containing beverages foods and are forbidden while doing the 5&1 diet plan. Certain fats are also not allowed, as well as all fried foods because they are high in saturated fats.

There are many types of foods that are not allowed for the 5&1 Diet Plan. These foods either contain high amounts of fats or carbohydrates that can contribute to weight gain. Below are the types of foods that are not allowed under this particular diet—unless included in the Fuels.

- Generous Desserts

Unsurprisingly, 5&1 dejects spoiling your sugar desires with sweets like ice cream, cakes, cookies and the likes.

Nevertheless, after the preliminary weight loss phase, reasonable sweet indulgences like freshly picked fruits or sweetened yogurt can be allowed their way back to your strict 5&1 diet.

- High Caloric Additions

Shortening, butter and elevated fat salad dressings increases flavor; however, they also increase large sums of calories. On 5&1, you will be advised to keep add-ons to a minimum or substitute lesser calorie forms.

- Alcohol

The Opt5&1 avia diet boosts customers to minimize alcohol consumption. If you are trying to stay within a stern calorie range, a 5-ounce glass of beer for 120 calories or the 150 calories in a 12-ounce glass of wine will add up fast.

- Fried and High-Fat Foods

Additionally, you cannot eat:

- Certain fats: butter, coconut oil, solid shortening.
- Whole fat dairy: milk, cheese, yogurt.
- Sugar-sweetened beverages: soda, fruit juice, sports drinks, energy drinks, sweet tea.
- Food allowed in the Maintenance Plan

The following foods will not be allowed while on the 5&1 Plan but added back through the 6-week transition phase and allowed during the 3&3 Plan:

- Fruit: all fresh fruit.
- Low in fat or fat-free dairy products: milk, cheese, yogurt.
- Total grains: total grain bread, high roughage breakfast cereal, brown or black or red rice, total wheat pasta.
- Legumes: lentils, soybeans, peas, beans.

CHAPTER 8
LEAN AND GREEN RECIPES

SALMON FLORENTINE

INGREDIENTS

- ½ cups of chopped cherry tomatoes
- ½ cup of chopped green onions
- garlic cloves, minced
- teaspoon of olive oil
- quantity of 12 oz. package frozen chopped spinach, thawed and patted dry
- ¼ teaspoon of crushed red pepper flakes
- ½ cup of part-skim ricotta cheese
- ¼ teaspoon each for pepper and salt
- quantities of 5 ½ oz. wild salmon fillets
- Cooking spray

DIRECTIONS

1. Preheat the oven to 3500F
2. Get a medium skillet to cook onions in oil until they start to soften, which should be in about 2 minutes. You can then add garlic inside the skillet and cook for an extra 1 minute. Add the spinach, red pepper flakes, tomatoes, pepper, and salt. Cook for 2 minutes while stirring. Remove the pan from the heat and let it cool for about 10 minutes. Stir in the ricotta
3. Put a quarter of the spinach mixture on top of each salmon fillet. Place the fillets on a slightly-greased rimmed baking sheet and bake it for 15 minutes or until you are sure that the salmon has been thoroughly cooked.

NUTRITIONS: Calories: 350 Carbohydrate: 15 g Protein: 42 g Fat: 13 g

TOMATO BRAISED CAULIFLOWER WITH CHICKEN

INGREDIENTS

- 4 garlic cloves, sliced
- 3 scallions, to be trimmed and cut into 1-inch pieces
- ¼ teaspoon of dried oregano
- ¼ teaspoon of crushed red pepper flakes
- 4 ½ cups of cauliflower
- 1 ½ cups of diced canned tomatoes
- 1 cup of fresh basil, gently torn
- ½ teaspoon each of pepper and salt, divided
- 1 ½ teaspoon of olive oil
- 1 ½ lb. of boneless, skinless chicken breasts

DIRECTIONS

1. Get a saucepan and combine the garlic, scallions, oregano, crushed red pepper, cauliflower, and tomato, and add ¼ cup of water. Get everything boil together and add ¼ teaspoon of pepper and salt for seasoning, then cover the pot with a lid. Let it simmer for 10 minutes and stir as often as possible until you observe that the cauliflower is tender. Now, wrap up the seasoning with the remaining ¼ teaspoon of pepper and salt.
2. Toss the chicken breast with oil, olive preferably and let it roast in the oven with the heat of 4500F for 20 minutes and an internal temperature of 1650F. Allow the chicken to rest for like 10 minutes.
3. Now slice the chicken, and serve on a bed of tomato braised cauliflower.

NUTRITIONS: Calories: 290 Fat: 10 g Carbohydrate: 13 g Protein: 38 g

BRAISED COLLARD GREENS IN PEANUT SAUCE WITH PORK TENDERLOIN

COOKING: 1 H 12' **PREPARATION:** 20' **SERVES:** 4

INGREDIENTS

- 2 cups of chicken stock
- 12 cups of chopped collard greens
- 5 tablespoon of powdered peanut butter
- 3 cloves of garlic, crushed
- 1 teaspoon of salt
- ½ teaspoon of allspice
- ½ teaspoon of black pepper
- 2 teaspoon of lemon juice
- ¾ teaspoon of hot sauce
- 1 ½ lb. of pork tenderloin

DIRECTIONS

1. Get a pot with a tight-fitting lid and combine the collards with the garlic, chicken stock, hot sauce, and half of the pepper and salt. Cook on low heat for about 1 hour or until the collards become tender.

2. Once the collards are tender, stir in the allspice, lemon juice. And powdered peanut butter. Keep warm.

3. Season the pork tenderloin with the remaining pepper and salt, and broil in a toaster oven for 10 minutes when you have an internal temperature of 1450F. Make sure to turn the tenderloin every 2 minutes to achieve an even browning all over. After that, you can take away the pork from the oven and allow it to rest for like 5 minutes.

4. Slice the pork as you will

NUTRITIONS: Calories: 320 Fat: 10 g Carbohydrate: 15 g Protein: 45 g

TOMATILLO AND GREEN CHILI PORK STEW

INGREDIENTS

- 2 scallions, chopped
- 2 cloves of garlic
- 1 lb. tomatillos, trimmed and chopped
- 8 large romaine or green lettuce leaves, divided
- 2 serrano chilies, seeds, and membranes
- ½ tsp of dried Mexican oregano (or you can use regular oregano)
- 1 ½ lb. of boneless pork loin, to be cut into bite-sized cubes
- ¼ cup of cilantro, chopped
- ¼ tablespoon (each) salt and paper
- 1 jalapeno, seeds and membranes to be removed and thinly sliced
- 1 cup of sliced radishes
- 4 lime wedges

DIRECTIONS

1. Combine scallions, garlic, tomatillos, 4 lettuce leaves, serrano chilies, and oregano in a blender. Then puree until smooth

2. Put pork and tomatillo mixture in a medium pot. 1-inch of puree should cover the pork; if not, add water until it covers it. Season with pepper & salt, and cover it simmers. Simmer on heat for approximately 20 minutes.

3. Now, finely shred the remaining lettuce leaves.

4. When the stew is done cooking, garnish with cilantro, radishes, finely shredded lettuce, sliced jalapenos, and lime wedges.

NUTRITIONS: Calories: 320 Protein: 44g Carbohydrate: 10g Fat: 11 g

RECIPES COOKBOOK FOR BEGINNERS

CLOUD BREAD

INGREDIENTS

- ½ cup of Fat-free 0% Plain Greek Yogurt (4.4 oz)
- 3 Eggs, Separated
- 16 teaspoon Cream of Tartar
- 1 Packet sweetener (a granulated sweetener just like stevia)

DIRECTIONS

1. For about 30 minutes before making this meal, place the Kitchen Aid Bowl and the whisk attachment in the freezer.
2. Preheat your oven to 30 degrees
3. Remove the mixing bowl and whisk attachment from the freezer
4. Separate the eggs. Now put the egg whites in the Kitchen Aid Bowl, and they should be in a different medium-sized bowl.
5. In the medium-sized bowl containing the yolks, mix in the sweetener and yogurt.
6. In the bowl containing the egg white, add in the cream of tartar. Beat this mixture until the egg whites turn to stiff peaks.
7. Now, take the egg yolk mixture and carefully fold it into the egg whites. Be cautious and avoid over-stirring.
8. Place baking paper on a baking tray and spray with cooking spray.
9. Scoop out 6 equally-sized "blobs" of the "dough" onto the parchment paper.
10. Bake for about 25-35 minutes (make sure you check when it is 25 minutes, in some ovens, they are done at this timestamp). You will know they are done as they will get brownish at the top and have some crack.
11. Most people like them cold against being warm
12. Most people like to re-heat in a toast oven or toaster to get them a little bit crispy.
13. Your serving size should be about 2 pieces.

NUTRITIONS: Calories: 234 Protein: 23g Carbs: 5g Fiber: 8g Sodium: 223g

AVOCADO LIME SHRIMP SALAD

INGREDIENTS

- 14 ounces of jumbo cooked shrimp, peeled and deveined; chopped
- 4 ½ ounces of avocado, diced
- 1 ½ cup of tomato, diced
- ¼ cup of chopped green onion
- ¼ cup of jalapeno with the seeds removed, diced fine
- 1 teaspoon of olive oil
- 2 tablespoons of lime juice
- 1/8 teaspoon of salt
- 1 tablespoon of chopped cilantro

DIRECTIONS

1. Get a small bowl and combine green onion, olive oil, lime juice, pepper, a pinch of salt. Wait for about 5 minutes for all of them to marinate and mellow the flavor of the onion.
2. Get a large bowl and combined chopped shrimp, tomato, avocado, jalapeno. Combine all of the ingredients, add cilantro, and gently toss.
3. Add pepper and salt as desired.

NUTRITIONS: Calories: 314 Protein: 26g Carbs: 15g Fiber: 9g

BROCCOLI CHEDDAR BREAKFAST BAKE

INGREDIENTS

- 9 eggs
- 6 cups of small broccoli florets
- ¼ teaspoon of salt
- 1 cup of unsweetened almond milk
- ¼ teaspoon of cayenne pepper
- ¼ teaspoon of ground pepper
- Cooking spray
- 4 oz. of shredded, reduced-fat cheddar

DIRECTIONS

1. Preheat your oven to about 375 degrees
2. In your large microwave-safe, add broccoli and 2 to 3 tablespoon of water. Microwave on high heat for 4 minutes or until it becomes tender. Now transfer the broccoli to a colander to drain excess liquid
3. Get a medium-sized bowl and whisk the milk, eggs, and seasonings together.
4. Set the broccoli neatly on the bottom of a lightly greased 13 x 9-inch baking dish. Sprinkle the cheese gently on the broccoli and pour the egg mixture on top of it.
5. Bake for about 45 minutes or until the center is set and the top forms a light brown crust.

NUTRITIONS: Calories: 290 Protein: 25g Carbohydrate: 8g Fat: 18 g

GRILLED MAHI MAHI WITH JICAMA SLAW

INGREDIENTS

- 1 teaspoon each for pepper and salt, divided
- 1 tablespoon of lime juice, divided
- 2 tablespoon + 2 teaspoons of extra virgin olive oil
- 4 raw mahi-mahi fillets, which should be about 8 oz. each
- ½ cucumber which should be thinly cut into long strips like matchsticks (it should yield about 1 cup)
- 1 jicama, which should be thinly cut into long strips like matchsticks (it should yield about 3 cups)
- 1 cup of alfalfa sprouts
- 2 cups of coarsely chopped watercress

DIRECTIONS

1. Combine ½ teaspoon of both pepper and salt, 1 teaspoon of lime juice, and 2 teaspoons of oil in a small bowl. Then brush the mahi-mahi fillets all through with the olive oil mixture.
2. Grill the mahi-mahi on medium-high heat until it becomes done in about 5 minutes, turn it to the other side, and let it be done for about 5 minutes. (You will have an internal temperature of about 145ºF).
3. For the slaw, combine the watercress, cucumber, jicama, and alfalfa sprouts in a bowl. Now combine ½ teaspoon of both pepper and salt, 2 teaspoons of lime juice, and 2 tablespoons of extra virgin oil in a small bowl. Drizzle it over slaw and toss together to combine.

NUTRITIONS: Calories: 320 Protein: 44g Carbohydrate: 10g Fat: 11 g

RECIPES COOKBOOK FOR BEGINNERS

ROSEMARY CAULIFLOWER ROLLS

INGREDIENTS

- 1/3 cup of almond flour
- 4 cups of riced cauliflower
- 1/3 cup of reduced-fat, shredded mozzarella or cheddar cheese
- 2 eggs
- 2 tablespoons of fresh rosemary, finely chopped
- ½ teaspoon of salt

DIRECTIONS

1. Preheat your oven to 4000F
2. Combine all the listed ingredients in a medium-sized bowl
3. Scoop cauliflower mixture into 12 evenly-sized rolls/biscuits onto a lightly-greased and foil-lined baking sheet.
4. Bake until it turns golden brown, which should be achieved in about 30 minutes.
5. Note: if you want to have the outside of the rolls/biscuits crisp, then broil for some minutes before serving.

NUTRITIONS: Calories: 254 Protein: 24g Carbohydrate: 7g Fat: 8 g

MEDITERRANEAN CHICKEN SALAD

INGREDIENTS

- For Chicken:
- 1 ¾ lb. boneless, skinless chicken breast
- ¼ teaspoon each of pepper and salt (or as desired)
- 1 ½ tablespoon of butter, melted
- For Mediterranean salad:
- 1 cup of sliced cucumber
- 6 cups of romaine lettuce, that is torn or roughly chopped
- 10 pitted Kalamata olives
- 1 pint of cherry tomatoes
- 1/3 cup of reduced-fat feta cheese
- ¼ teaspoon each of pepper and salt (or lesser)
- 1 small lemon juice (it should be about 2 tablespoons)

DIRECTIONS

1. Preheat your oven or grill to about 3500F.
2. Season the chicken with salt, butter, and black pepper
3. Roast or grill chicken until it reaches an internal temperature of 1650F in about 25 minutes. Once your chicken breasts are cooked, remove and keep aside to rest for about 5 minutes before you slice it.
4. Combine all the salad ingredients you have and toss everything together very well
5. Serve the chicken with Mediterranean salad

NUTRITIONS: Calories: 290 Fat: 10 g Carbohydrate: 13 g Protein: 38 g

CHAPTER 9
FUELING RECIPES

FUELING MOUSSE

INGREDIENTS

- 1 packet hot cocoa
- 1/2 cup sugar-free gelatin
- 1 tablespoon light cream cheese
- 2 tablespoons cold water
- 1/4 cup crushed ice

DIRECTIONS

1. Place all ingredients in a blender.
2. Pulse until smooth.
3. Pour into glass and place in the fridge to set.
4. Serve chilled.

NUTRITIONS: Calories per serving: 156 Cal Protein: 5.7 g Carbs: 17.6 g Fat: 3.7 g Sugar: 4.5 g

BAKED CHEESY EGGPLANT

INGREDIENTS

- Eggplant (1, fresh)
- Tomato (1, 16 can, chopped)
- Tomato sauce (2, 8 oz. can)
- Cheddar cheese (6 oz., shredded)
- Onion (1, chopped)
- Oregano (dash, dried)
- Salt (2 tsp.)
- Italian seasoning (dash)
- Basil (dried, for taste)
- Thyme (dried, for flavor)
- Garlic (2-3 tsp., powdered)
- Black pepper (1/2 tsp.)

DIRECTIONS

1. Slice eggplant (fresh) into thin slices then season using a dash of salt.
2. Next, set aside in a colander for roughly 30 minutes then pat dry using a few paper towels.
3. Rinse under warm running water and thoroughly slice eggplant into quarters.
4. Place a layer of the eggplant (quartered) into a baking dish (large).
5. Cover layer using the tomatoes (chopped) and tomato sauce (1 can).
6. Add 1/2 of the cheese over the top and repeat layers with the remaining cheese (shredded) over the top.
7. Place eggplant into the oven to bake for approximately 45 minutes at 350 degrees Fahrenheit until eggplant is soft.

NUTRITIONS: Protein: 11.7 g Carbohydrates: 15.4 g Dietary Fiber: 5.4 g

TABASCO ANZAC

INGREDIENTS

- 85g porridge oats
- 85g desiccated coconut
- 85g sultanas
- 100g plain flour
- 100g caster sugar
- 100g butter
- 1 tbsp. golden syrup
- 2 tsp. Tabasco
- 2 tbsp. hot water
- 1 tsp. bicarbonate of soda

DIRECTIONS

1. Preheat fan assisted oven to 350F.
2. Positioned the oats, raisins, coconut, flour, and sugar in a bowl.
3. Soften the butter in a small pan and stir inside the golden syrup, Tabasco sauce, and water.
4. Add the bicarbonate of soda and mix well.
5. Add the liquid to the bowl and mix well until all the ingredients are combined.
6. Using a dessert spoon, spoon the mixture onto a buttered baking sheet. Leave about 2.5cm in-between each spoonful to allow room for spreading.
7. Bake in batches for 8-10 minutes until golden.
8. Place the cooked biscuits onto a wire rack to cool.

NUTRITIONS: Fat: 41 g Protein: 12 g Cholesterol: 20 mg Carbohydrates: 20 g Sodium: 504 mg

SWEET POTATO CASSEROLE

INGREDIENTS

- Potatoes (3 lbs., sweet, peeled, chopped)
- Greek yogurt (1 cup, nonfat)
- Cinnamon (1/2 tbsp, ground)
- Nutmeg (1/8 tsp., ground)
- Sea salt (1/4 tsp.)
- Egg whites (6 tbsp)
- Butter (1 tbsp, melted)
- Pecans (1/2 cup, chopped)
- Marshmallows (1/2 cup, miniature)
- Sugar (dash, light brown, for sprinkling)

DIRECTIONS

1. Heat your oven to 375 degrees Fahrenheit.
2. Place the potatoes (sweet) into a saucepan (large) over medium high heat.
3. Cover potatoes using water then bring to a boil, boil for approximately 30 minutes until soft.
4. Drain potatoes then place potatoes back into the saucepan.
5. Add the Greek yogurt, cinnamon (ground), nutmeg (base) and sea salt (dash) into the potatoes.
6. Stir well until coated (evenly).
7. Add in the butter (melted) and egg whites then bring to a stir once more.
8. Transfer potato mixture into a casserole dish (large).
9. Place into oven then bake for approximately 30 minutes. Remove from heat then top with the pecans (chopped) and miniature marshmallows.
10. Place back into oven to bake for an additional 10 minutes until marshmallows are browned.

NUTRITIONS: Protein: 2.9 g Carbohydrates: 30.1 g Dietary Fiber: 1.9 g

EASTER BUNNY

INGREDIENTS

- 170 g butter
- 1 1/4 cups icing sugar mixture
- 1 tsp. vanilla extract
- 1 pinch salt
- 3 egg yolks
- 2 1/2 cups plain flour
- 12 marshmallows
- 24 Nestle Smarties pink
- 72 Ferrero Tic Tacs pink
- 3 drops liquid food coloring pink
- Royal Icing
- 2 egg whites
- 2 tsp. lemon juice
- 3 cups icing sugar sifted

DIRECTIONS

1. Preheat the oven to a hundred and 158F.
2. Whisk the butter using hand until it is smooth and creamy.
3. Blend within the icing sugar then add the egg yolks, vanilla, and salt. Stir until blended.
4. Add the flour and blend it loosely with a wooden spoon till the dough comes together.
5. Turn it out onto a floured surface and knead until the dough is smooth.
6. Shape it into a disc and wrap it in cling wrap.
7. Refrigerate the dough for 30 minutes.
8. Roll out the dough to about 1 cm thick. Use a 5-6cm round cookie cutter to cut 12 bunny butt shapes out of the dough. Then use a small egg-shaped cookie cutter to create 24 bunny feet.
9. Place the cookies onto two baking trays lined with baking paper.
10. Bake in the oven for 10-15 minutes until the edges turned browned.
11. Cool on a cooling rack while you make some royal icing.
12. Divide the icing into two halves. Color one half with a few drops of rose food coloring to make it very light bunny pink.
13. Ice half of your biscuits with pink and half white. Add two bunny's feet to each circle. Add a marshmallow tail and then a Smartie as a paw pad and three tic tacs for the paw toes.
14. Icing:
15. The use of an electric powered mixer, whisk egg whites with the lemon juice till blended.
16. Regularly upload in sifted icing sugar on low pace till clean.
17. Add meals color of your preference.
18. Pipe onto bunny biscuits.
19. Leave for 2-3 hours to set difficult.

NUTRITIONS: Fat: 41 g Protein: 12 g Cholesterol: 20 mg Carbohydrates: 20 g Sodium: 504 mg

HIGH PROTEIN CHIPOTLE CHEDDAR QUESADILLA

INGREDIENTS

- Tortillas (4, low carb)
- Cottage cheese (2 cups, low sodium)
- Cheddar cheese (2 cups, low fat, shredded)
- Bell pepper (1, red, thinly sliced)
- Onion (1, thinly sliced)
- Portobello mushrooms (1 cup, thinly sliced)
- Chipotle seasoning (2-3 tbsp)
- Mild salsa (for dipping)

DIRECTIONS

1. Add the bell pepper (sliced, red), onion (sliced) and mushrooms (sliced) into a large grill pan over medium heat.
2. Cook for approximately 10 minutes until soft. Remove then transfer into a bowl (medium). Set aside.
3. Add the chipotle seasoning and cottage cheese in a small bowl. Stir well to incorporate.
4. Place tortillas onto the grill pan and pour vegetable mixture over tortillas.
5. Sprinkle cottage cheese mixture over the top then top off using the cheddar cheese (shredded).
6. Place an additional tortilla over the top of filling.
7. Cook for roughly 2 minutes then flip and continue cooking for a next minute.
8. Repeat process with remaining tortillas and filling.
9. Serve immediately with the salsa (mild).

NUTRITIONS: Calories: 287 Cal Protein: 32.6 g Carbohydrates: 29.8 g Fats: 10.6 g

ZUCCHINI BOATS WITH BEEF AND PIMIENTO ROJO

INGREDIENTS

- 4 zucchinis
- 2 tbsp olive oil
- 1 1/2 lb. ground beef
- 1 medium red onion, chopped
- 2 tbsp chopped pimiento
- Pink salt and black pepper to taste
- 1 cup grated yellow cheddar cheese

DIRECTIONS

1. Preheat oven to 350°F.
2. Lay the zucchinis on a flat surface, trim off the ends and cut in half lengthwise. Scoop out the pulp from each half with a spoon to make shells. Chop the pulp.
3. Heat oil in a skillet; add the ground beef, red onion, pimiento, zucchini pulp, and season with salt and black pepper.
4. Cook for 6 minutes while stirring to break up lumps until beef is no longer pink. Turn the heat off.
5. Spoon the beef into the boats and sprinkle with cheddar cheese.
6. Place on a greased baking sheet and cook to melt the cheese for 15 minutes until zucchini boats are tender.
7. Take out, cool for 2 minutes, and serve warm with a mixed green salad.

NUTRITIONS: Calories: 335 Cal Fats: 24 g Carbohydrates: 7 g Protein: 18 g

AVOCADO SHRIMP CUCUMBERBITES

INGREDIENTS

- » 1 large cucumber, cut into thick circles
- » 6 small shrimp
- » 1/2 cup parmesan cheese, grated
- » 1 tsp. almond butter, cubed
- » Salt and pepper to taste
- » 1 tsp. coriander, chopped

DIRECTIONS

1. Preheat the oven to 390 degrees F.
2. Add wax paper on a baking sheet.
3. Arrange the cucumber pieces on the baking sheet.
4. Add one shrimp on each slice.
5. Add the butter cubes, cheese, salt, pepper, and coriander on top.
6. Bake for 10 minutes. Serve.

NUTRITIONS: Fat: 2g Cholesterol: 51 mg Sodium: 240 mg Potassium: 83 mg Carbohydrates: 1 g Protein: 4 g

CRISPY CAULIFLOWERS

INGREDIENTS

- » 2 cup cauliflower florets, diced
- » 1/2 cup almond flour
- » 1/2 cup coconut flour
- » Salt and pepper to taste
- » 1 tsp. mixed herbs
- » 1 tsp. chives, chopped
- » 1 egg
- » 1 tsp. cumin
- » 1/2 tsp. garlic powder
- » 1 cup water
- » Oil for frying

DIRECTIONS

1. Combine the egg, salt, garlic, water, cumin, chives, mixed herbs, pepper, and flour in a mixing bowl.
2. Add the cauliflower in the mixture and then fry them in oil until they become golden in color.
3. Serve.

NUTRITIONS: Protein: 3.3 g Carbohydrates: 19.4 g Fiber: 1.3 g Fat: 10.4 g

STRAWBERRY-AVOCADO TOAST WITH BALSAMIC GLAZE

COOKING: 30'   **PREPARATION: 5'**   **SERVES: 4**

INGREDIENTS

- 1 avocado, peeled, pitted, and quartered
- 4 whole-wheat bread slices, toasted
- 4 ripe strawberries, cut into 1/4-inch slices
- 1 tablespoon balsamic glaze or reduction

DIRECTIONS

1. Mash one-quarter of the avocado on a slice of toast.
2. Layer one-quarter of the strawberry slices over the avocado, and finish with a drizzle of balsamic glaze.
3. Repeat with the remaining ingredients, and serve.
4. Tip: If you can't buy balsamic glaze, make your own! Put balsamic vinegar in a small saucepan and cook, uncovered, over low heat for roughly 45 minutes, or until it's reduced to nearly one-quarter of the original amount of liquid.

NUTRITIONS: Fat: 8 g Carbohydrates: 17 g Fiber: 5 g Protein: 5 g

CHAPTER 10.
FUELING RECIPES 2

TROPICAL GREENS SMOOTHIE

INGREDIENTS

- One banana
- 1/2 large navel orange, peeled and segmented
- 1/2 cup frozen mango chunks
- 1 cup frozen spinach
- One celery stalk, broken into pieces
- One tablespoon cashew butter or almond butter
- 1/2 tablespoon spiraling
- 1/2 tablespoon ground flaxseed
- 1/2 cup unsweetened nondairy milk
- Water, for thinning (optional)

DIRECTIONS

1. In a high-speed blender or food processor, combine the bananas, orange, mango, spinach, celery, cashew butter, spiraling (if using), flaxseed, and milk.
2. Blend until creamy, adding more milk or water to thin the smoothie if too thick. Serve immediately—it is best served fresh.

NUTRITIONS: Calories: 391 Fat: 12g Protein: 13g Carbohydrates: 68g Fiber: 13g

VITAMIN C SMOOTHIE CUBES

INGREDIENTS

- 1/8 large papaya
- 1/8 mango
- 1/4 cups chopped pineapple, fresh or frozen
- 1/8 cup raw cauliflower florets, fresh or frozen
- 1/4 large navel oranges, peeled and halved
- 1/4 large orange bell pepper stemmed, seeded, and coarsely chopped

DIRECTIONS

1. Halve the papaya and mango, remove the pits, and scoop their soft flesh into a high-speed blender.
2. Add the pineapple, cauliflower, oranges, and bell pepper. Blend until smooth.
3. Evenly divide the puree between 2 (16-compartment) ice cube trays and place them on a level surface in your freezer. Freeze for at least 8 hours.
4. The cubes can be left in the ice cube trays until use or transferred to a freezer bag. The frozen cubes are good for about three weeks in a standard freezer or up to 6 months in a chest freezer.

NUTRITIONS: Calories: 96 Fat: <1g Protein: 2g Carbohydrates: 24g Fiber: 4g

OVERNIGHT CHOCOLATE CHIA PUDDING

COOKING: OVERNIGHT TO CHILL   PREPARATION: 2'   SERVES: 1

INGREDIENTS

- 1/8 cup chia seeds
- 1/2 cup unsweetened nondairy milk
- One tablespoon raw cacao powder
- 1/2 teaspoon vanilla extract
- 1/2 teaspoon pure maple syrup

DIRECTIONS

1. Stir together the chia seeds, milk, cacao powder, vanilla, and maple syrup in a large bowl. Divide between 2 (1/2-pint) covered glass jars or containers. Refrigerate overnight.
2. Stir before serving.

NUTRITIONS: Calories: 213 Fat: 10g Protein: 9g Carbohydrates: 20g Fiber: 15g

SLOW COOKER SAVORY BUTTERNUT SQUASH OATMEAL

COOKING: 6-8 H   PREPARATION: 15'   SERVES: 1

INGREDIENTS

- 1/4 cup steel-cut oats
- 1/2 cups cubed (1/2-inch pieces) peeled butternut squash (freeze any leftovers after preparing a whole squash for future meals)
- 3/4 cups of water
- 1/16 cup unsweetened nondairy milk
- 1/4 tablespoon chia seed
- 1/2 teaspoons yellow (mellow) miso paste
- 3/4 teaspoons ground ginger
- 1/4 tablespoon sesame seed, toasted
- 1/4 tablespoon chopped scallion, green parts only
- Shredded carrot, for serving (optional)

DIRECTIONS

1. In a slow cooker, combine the oats, butternut squash, and water.
2. Cover the slow cooker and cook on low for 6 to 8 hours, or until the squash is fork tender. Using a potato masher or heavy spoon, roughly mash the cooked butternut squash. Stir to combine with the oats.
3. Whisk together the milk, chia seeds, miso paste, and ginger to combine in a large bowl. Stir the mixture into the oats.
4. Top your oatmeal bowl with sesame seeds and scallion for more plant-based fiber, top with shredded carrot (if using).

NUTRITIONS: Calories: 471 Fat: 16g Protein: 18g Carbohydrates: 69g Fiber: 16g

CARROT CAKE OATMEAL

INGREDIENTS

- 1/8 cup pecans
- 1/2 cup finely shredded carrot
- 1/4 cup old-fashioned oats
- 5/8 cups unsweetened nondairy milk
- 1/2 tablespoon pure maple syrup
- 1/2 teaspoon ground cinnamon
- 1/2 teaspoon ground ginger
- 1/8 teaspoon ground nutmeg
- One tablespoon chia seed

DIRECTIONS

1. Over medium-high heat in a skillet, toast the pecans for 3 to 4 minutes, often stirring, until browned and fragrant (watch closely, as they can burn quickly). Pour the pecans onto a cutting board and coarsely chop them. Set aside.

2. In an 8-quart pot over medium-high heat, combine the carrot, oats, milk, maple syrup, cinnamon, ginger, and nutmeg. When it is already boiling, reduce the heat to medium-low. Cook, uncovered, for 10 minutes, stirring occasionally.

3. Stir in the chopped pecans and chia seeds. Serve immediately.

NUTRITIONS: Calories: 307 Fat: 17g Protein: 7g Carbohydrates: 35g Fiber: 11g

SPICED SORGHUM AND BERRIES

INGREDIENTS

- 1/4 cup whole-grain sorghum
- 1/4 teaspoon ground cinnamon
- 1/4 teaspoon Chinese five-spice powder
- 3/4 cups water
- 1/4 cup unsweetened nondairy milk
- 1/4 teaspoon vanilla extract
- 1/2 tablespoons pure maple syrup
- 1/2 tablespoon chia seed
- 1/8 cup sliced almonds
- 1/2 cups fresh raspberries, divided

DIRECTIONS

1. Using a large pot over medium-high heat, stir together the sorghum, cinnamon, five-spice powder, and water. Wait for the water to a boil, cover the bank, and reduce the heat to medium-low. Cook for 1 hour, or until the sorghum is soft and chewy. If the sorghum grains are still hard, add another water cup and cook for 15 minutes more.

2. Using a glass measuring cup, whisk together the milk, vanilla, and maple syrup to blend. Add the mixture to the sorghum and the chia seeds, almonds, and 1 cup of raspberries. Gently stir to combine.

3. When serving, top with the remaining 1 cup of fresh raspberries.

NUTRITIONS: Calories: 289 Fat: 8g Protein: 9g Carbohydrates: 52g Fiber: 53g

RAW-CINNAMON-APPLE NUT BOWL

INGREDIENTS

- One green apple halved, seeded, and cored
- 3/4 Honey crisp apples, halved, seeded, and cored
- 1/4 teaspoon freshly squeezed lemon juice
- One pitted Medrol dates
- 1/8 teaspoon ground cinnamon
- Pinch ground nutmeg
- 1/2 tablespoons chia seeds, plus more for serving (optional)
- 1/4 tablespoon hemp seed
- 1/8 cup chopped walnuts
- Nut butter, for serving (optional)

DIRECTIONS

1. Finely dice half the green apple and 1 Honey crisp apple. With the lemon juice, store it in an airtight container while you work on the next steps.

2. Coarsely chop the remaining apples and the dates. Transfer to a food processor and add the cinnamon and nutmeg. Check it several times if it combines, then processes for 2 to 3 minutes to puree. Stir the puree into the reserved diced apples. Stir in the chia seeds (if using), hemp seeds, and walnuts. Chill for at least 1 hour. Enjoy!

3. Serve as is or top with additional chia seeds and nut butter (if using).

NUTRITIONS: Calories: 274 Fat: 8g Protein: 4g Carbohydrates: 52g Fiber: 9g

PEANUT BUTTER AND CACAO BREAKFAST QUINOA

INGREDIENTS

- 1/3 cup quinoa flakes
- 1/2 cup unsweetened nondairy milk,
- 1/2 cup of water
- 1/8 cup raw cacao powder
- One tablespoon natural creamy peanut butter
- 1/8 teaspoon ground cinnamon
- One banana, mashed
- Fresh berries of choice, for serving
- Chopped nuts of choice, for serving

DIRECTIONS

1. Using an 8-quart pot over medium-high heat, stir together the quinoa flakes, milk, water, cacao powder, peanut butter, and cinnamon. Cook and stir it until the mixture begins to simmer. Turn the heat to medium-low and cook for 3 to 5 minutes, stirring frequently.

2. Stir in the bananas and cook until hot.

3. Serve topped with fresh berries, nuts, and a splash of milk.

NUTRITIONS: Calories: 471 Fat: 16g Protein: 18g Carbohydrates: 69g Fiber: 16g

VANILLA BUCKWHEAT PORRIDGE

INGREDIENTS

- One cup of water
- 1/4 cup raw buckwheat grouts
- 1/4 teaspoon ground cinnamon
- 1/4 banana, sliced
- 1/16 cup golden raisins
- 1/16 cup dried currants
- 1/16 cup sunflower seeds
- 1/2 tablespoons chia seeds
- 1/4 tablespoon hemp seed
- 1/4 tablespoon sesame seed, toasted
- 1/8 cup unsweetened nondairy milk
- 1/4 tablespoon pure maple syrup
- 1/4 teaspoon vanilla extract

DIRECTIONS

1. Boil the water in a pot. Stir in the buckwheat, cinnamon, and banana. Cook the mixture. Mixing it and wait for it to boil, then reduce the heat to medium-low. Cover the pot and cook for 15 minutes, or until the buckwheat is tender. Remove from the heat.

2. Stir in the raisins, currants, sunflower seeds, chia seeds, hemp seeds, sesame seeds, milk, maple syrup, and vanilla. Cover the pot. Wait for 10 minutes before serving.

3. Serve as is or top as desired.

NUTRITIONS: Calories: 353 Fat: 11g Protein: 10g Carbohydrates: 61g Fiber: 10g

POLENTA WITH SEARED PEARS

INGREDIENTS

- One cup water, divided, plus more as needed
- 1/2 cups coarse cornmeal
- One tablespoon pure maple syrup
- 1/4 tablespoon molasses
- 1/4 teaspoon ground cinnamon
- 1/2 ripe pears, cored and diced
- 1/4 cup fresh cranberries
- 1/4 teaspoon chopped fresh rosemary leaves

DIRECTIONS

1. In a pan, cook 5 cups of water to a simmer.

2. While whisking continuously to avoid clumping, slowly pour in the cornmeal. Cook, often stirring with a heavy spoon, for 30 minutes. The polenta should be thick and creamy.

3. While the polenta cooks, in a saucepan over medium heat, stir together the maple syrup, molasses, the remaining 1/4 cup of water, and the cinnamon until combined. Bring it to a simmer. Add the pears and cranberries. Cook for 10 minutes, occasionally stirring, until the pears are tender and start to brown. Remove from the heat. Stir in the rosemary and let the mixture sit for 5 minutes. If it is too thick, add another 1/4 cup of water and return to the heat.

4. Top with the cranberry-pear mixture.

NUTRITIONS: Calories: 282 Fat: 2g Protein: 4g Carbohydrates: 65g Fiber: 12g

BEST WHOLE WHEAT PANCAKES

INGREDIENTS

- 3/4 tablespoons ground flaxseed
- Two tablespoons warm water
- 1/2 cups whole wheat pastry flour
- 1/8 cup rye flour
- 1/2 tablespoons double-acting baking powder
- 1/4 teaspoon ground cinnamon
- 1/8 teaspoon ground ginger
- One cup unsweetened nondairy milk
- 3/4 tablespoons pure maple syrup
- 1/4 teaspoon vanilla extract

DIRECTIONS

1. Mix the warm water and flaxseed in a large bowl. Set aside for at least 5 minutes.
2. Whisk together the pastry and rye flours, baking powder, cinnamon, and ginger to combine.
3. Whisk together the milk, maple syrup, and vanilla in a large bowl. Make use of a spatula, fold the wet ingredients into the dry ingredients. Fold in the soaked flaxseed until fully incorporated.
4. Heat a large skillet or nonstick griddle over medium-high heat. Working in batches, 3 to 4 pancakes at a time, add 1/4-cup portions of batter to the hot skillet. Until golden brown, cook for 3 to 4 minutes each side or no liquid batter is visible.

NUTRITIONS: Calories: 301 Fat: 4g Protein: 10g Carbohydrates: 57g Fiber: 10g

SPICED PUMPKIN MUFFINS

INGREDIENTS

- 1/6 tablespoons ground flaxseed
- 1/24 cup of water
- 1/8 cups whole wheat flour
- 1/6 teaspoons baking powder
- 5/6 teaspoons ground cinnamon
- 1/12 teaspoon baking soda
- 1/12 teaspoon ground ginger
- 1/16 teaspoon ground nutmeg
- 1/32 teaspoon ground cloves
- 1/6 cup pumpkin puree
- 1/12 cup pure maple syrup
- 1/24 cup unsweetened applesauce
- 1/24 cup unsweetened nondairy milk
- 1/2 teaspoons vanilla extract

DIRECTIONS

1. Preheat the oven to 350°F. Line a 12-cup metal muffin pan with parchment paper liners or use a silicone muffin pan.
2. First, mix the flaxseed and water in a large bowl then keep it aside.
3. In a medium bowl, stir together the flour, baking powder, cinnamon, baking soda, ginger, nutmeg, and cloves.
4. In a medium bowl, stir up the maple syrup, pumpkin puree, applesauce, milk, and vanilla. Crease the wet ingredients into the dry ingredients make use of a spatula.
5. Fold the soaked flaxseed into the batter until evenly combined, but do not over mix the batter, or your muffins will become dense. Spoon about 1/4 cup of batter per muffin into your prepared muffin pan.
6. Bake for 18 to 20 minutes, or until a toothpick inserted into the center of a muffin comes out clean. Remove the muffins from the pan.
7. Transfer to a wire rack for cooling.
8. Store in an airtight container that is at room temperature.

NUTRITIONS: Calories: 115 Fat: 1g Protein: 3g Carbohydrates: 25g Fiber: 3g

CHAPTER 11.
BREAKFAST

PIZZA HACK

INGREDIENTS

- 1/4 fueling of garlic mashed potato
- 1/2 egg whites
- 1/4 tablespoon of Baking powder
- 3/4 oz. of reduced-fat shredded mozzarella
- 1/8 cup of sliced white mushrooms
- 1/16 cup of pizza sauce
- 3/4 oz. of ground beef
- 1/4 sliced black olives
- You also need a sauté pan, baking sheets, and parchment paper

DIRECTIONS

1. Start by preheating the oven to 400°
2. Mix your baking powder and garlic potato packet
3. Add egg whites to your mixture and stir well until it blends.
4. Line the baking sheet with parchment paper and pour the mixed batter onto it
5. Put another parchment paper on top of the batter and spread out the batter to a 1/8-inch circle.
6. Then place another baking sheet on top; this way, the matter is between two baking sheets.
7. Place into an oven and bake for about 8 minutes until the pizza crust is golden brown.
8. For the toppings, place your ground beef in a sauté pan and fry till its brown, and wash your mushrooms very well.
9. After the crust is baked, remove the top layer of parchment paper carefully to prevent the form from sticking to the pizza crust.
10. Put your toppings on top of the crust and bake for an extra 8 minutes.
11. Once ready, slide the pizza off the parchment paper and into a plate.

NUTRITIONS: Calories: 478 Protein: 30 g Carbohydrates: 22 g Fats: 29 g

SWEET CASHEW CHEESE SPREAD

INGREDIENTS

- Stevia (5 drops)
- Cashews (2 cups, raw)
- Water (1/2 cup)

DIRECTIONS

1. Soak the cashews overnight in water.
2. Next, drain the excess water then transfer cashews to a food processor.
3. Add in the stevia and the water.
4. Process until smooth.
5. Serve chilled. Enjoy.

NUTRITIONS: Fat: 7 g Cholesterol 0 mg Sodium 12.6 mg Carbohydrates 5.7 g

MINI ZUCCHINI BITES

INGREDIENTS

- 1 zucchini, cut into thick circles
- 3 cherry tomatoes, halved
- 1/2 cup parmesan cheese, grated
- Salt and pepper to taste
- 1 tsp. chives, chopped

DIRECTIONS

1. Preheat the oven to 390 degrees F.
2. Add wax paper on a baking sheet.
3. Arrange the zucchini pieces.
4. Add the cherry halves on each zucchini slice.
5. Add parmesan cheese, chives, and sprinkle with salt and pepper.
6. Bake for 10 minutes. Serve.

NUTRITIONS: Fat: 1.0 g Cholesterol: 5.0 mg Sodium: 400.3 mg Potassium: 50.5 mg Carbohydrates: 7.3 g

WHOLE-WHEAT BLUEBERRY MUFFINS

INGREDIENTS

- 1/2 cup plant-based milk
- 1/2 cup unsweetened applesauce
- 1/2 cup maple syrup
- 1 teaspoon vanilla extract
- 2 cups whole-wheat flour
- 1/2 teaspoon baking soda
- 1 cup blueberries

DIRECTIONS

1. Preheat the oven to 375°F.
2. In a large bowl, mix the milk, applesauce, maple syrup, and vanilla.
3. Stir in the flour and baking soda until no dry flour is left and the batter is smooth.
4. Gently fold in the blueberries until they are evenly distributed throughout the batter.
5. In a muffin tin, fill 8 muffin cups three-quarters full of batter.
6. Bake for 25 minutes, or until you can stick a knife into the center of a muffin and it comes out clean. Allow to cool before serving.
7. Tip: Both frozen and fresh blueberries will work great in this recipe. The only difference will be that muffins using fresh blueberries will cook slightly quicker than those using frozen.

NUTRITIONS: Fat: 1 g Carbohydrates: 45 g Fiber: 2 g Protein: 4 g

WALNUT CRUNCH BANANA BREAD

INGREDIENTS

- 4 ripe bananas
- 1/4 cup maple syrup
- 1 tablespoon apple cider vinegar
- 1 teaspoon vanilla extract
- 1 1/2 cups whole-wheat flour
- 1/2 teaspoon ground cinnamon
- 1/2 teaspoon baking soda
- 1/4 cup walnut pieces (optional)

DIRECTIONS

1. Preheat the oven to 350°F.
2. In a large bowl, use a fork or mixing spoon to mash the bananas until they reach a puréed consistency (small bits of banana are acceptable). Stir in the maple syrup, apple cider vinegar, and vanilla.
3. Stir in the flour, cinnamon, and baking soda. Fold in the walnut pieces (if using).
4. Gently pour the batter into a loaf pan, filling it no more than three-quarters of the way full. Bake for 1 hour, or until you can stick a knife into the middle and it comes out clean.
5. Remove from the oven and allow cooling on the countertop for a minimum of 30 minutes before serving.

NUTRITIONS: Fat: 1g Carbohydrates: 40 g Fiber: 5 g Protein: 4 g

PLANT-POWERED PANCAKES

INGREDIENTS

- 1 cup whole-wheat flour
- 1 teaspoon baking powder
- 1/2 teaspoon ground cinnamon
- 1 cup plant-based milk
- 1/2 cup unsweetened applesauce
- 1/4 cup maple syrup
- 1 teaspoon vanilla extract

DIRECTIONS

1. In a large bowl, combine the flour, baking powder, and cinnamon.
2. Stir in the milk, applesauce, maple syrup, and vanilla until no dry flour is left and the batter is smooth.
3. Heat a large, nonstick skillet or griddle over medium heat. For each pancake, pour 1/4 cup of batter onto the hot skillet. Once bubbles form over the top of the pancake and the sides begin to brown, flip and cook for 1 to 2 minutes more.
4. Repeat until all of the batter is used, and serve.

NUTRITIONS: Fat: 2 g Carbohydrates: 44 g Fiber: 5 g Protein: 5 g

SHAKE CAKE FUELING

INGREDIENTS

- One packet of Optavia shakes.
- 1/4 teaspoon of baking powder
- Two tablespoons of eggbeaters or egg whites
- Two tablespoons of water
- Other options that are not compulsory include sweetener, reduced-fat cream cheese, etc.

DIRECTIONS

1. Begin by preheating the oven.
2. Mix all the ingredients begin with the dry ingredients first before adding the wet ingredients.
3. After the mixture/batter is ready, pour gently into muffin cups.
4. Inside the oven, place, and bake for about 16-18 minutes or until it is baked and ready. Allow it to cool completely.
5. Add additional toppings of your choice and ensure your delicious shake cake is refreshing.

NUTRITIONS: Calories: 896 Fat: 37 g Carbohydrate: 115 g Protein: 34 g

BISCUIT PIZZA

INGREDIENTS

- 1/4 sachet of buttermilk cheddar and herb biscuit
- 1/4 tablespoon of tomato sauce
- 1/4 tablespoon of low-fat shredded cheese
- 1/4 table of water
- Parchment paper

DIRECTIONS

1. You may begin by preheating the oven to about 350°F
2. Mix the biscuit and water and stir properly.
3. In the parchment paper, pour the mixture and spread it into a thin circle. Allow cooking for 10 minutes.
4. Take it out and add the tomato sauce and shredded cheese.
5. Bake it for a few more minutes.

NUTRITIONS: Calories: 478 Protein: 30 g Carbohydrates: 22 g Fats: 29 g

RECIPES COOKBOOK FOR BEGINNERS

MINI MAC IN A BOWL

INGREDIENTS

- 5 ounce of lean ground beef
- Two tablespoons of diced white or yellow onion.
- 1/8 teaspoon of onion powder
- 1/8 teaspoon of white vinegar
- 1 ounce of dill pickle slices
- One teaspoon sesame seed
- 3 cups of shredded Romaine lettuce
- Cooking spray
- Two tablespoons reduced-fat shredded cheddar cheese
- Two tablespoons of Wish-bone light thousand island as dressing

DIRECTIONS

1. Place a lightly greased small skillet on fire to heat,
2. Add your onion to cook for about 2-3 minutes,
3. Next, add the beef and allow cooking until it's brown
4. Next, mix your vinegar and onion powder with the dressing,
5. Finally, top the lettuce with the cooked meat and sprinkle cheese on it, add your pickle slices.
6. Drizzle the mixture with the sauce and sprinkle the sesame seeds also.
7. Your mini mac in a bowl is ready for consumption.

NUTRITIONS: Calories: 150 Protein: 21 g Carbohydrates: 32 g Fats: 19 g

LEAN AND GREEN SMOOTHIE 1

INGREDIENTS

- 2 1/2 cups of kale leaves
- 3/4 cup of chilled apple juice
- 1 cup of cubed pineapple
- 1/2 cup of frozen green grapes
- 1/2 cup of chopped apple

DIRECTIONS

1. Place the pineapple, apple juice, apple, frozen seedless grapes, and kale leaves in a blender.
2. Cover and blend until it's smooth.
3. Smoothie is ready and can be garnished with halved grapes if you wish.

NUTRITIONS: Calories: 81 Protein: 2 g Carbohydrates: 19 g Fats: 1 g

LEAN AND GREEN SMOOTHIE 2

INGREDIENTS

- Six kale leaves
- Two peeled oranges
- 2 cups of mango kombucha
- 2 cups of chopped pineapple
- 2 cups of water

DIRECTIONS

1. Break up the oranges, place in the blender,
2. Add the mango kombucha, chopped pineapple, and kale leaves into the blender
3. Blend everything until it is smooth.
4. Smoothie is ready to be taken.

NUTRITIONS: Calories: 81 Protein: 2 g Carbohydrates: 19 g Fats: 1 g

LEAN AND GREEN CHICKEN PESTO PASTA

INGREDIENTS

- 3 cups of raw kale leaves
- 2 tbsp. of olive oil
- 2 cups of fresh basil
- 1/4 teaspoon salt
- 3 tbsp. lemon juice
- Three garlic cloves
- 2 cups of cooked chicken breast
- 1 cup of baby spinach
- 6 ounce of uncooked chicken pasta
- 3 ounces of diced fresh mozzarella
- Basil leaves or red pepper flakes to garnish

DIRECTIONS

1. Start by making the pesto, add the kale, lemon juice, basil, garlic cloves, olive oil, and salt to a blender and blend until its smooth.
2. Add salt and pepper to taste.
3. Cook the pasta and strain off the water. Reserve 1/4 cup of the liquid.
4. Get a bowl and mix everything, the cooked pasta, pesto, diced chicken, spinach, mozzarella, and the reserved pasta liquid.
5. Sprinkle the mixture with additional chopped basil or red paper flakes (optional).
6. Now your salad is ready. You may serve it warm or chilled. Also, it can be taken as a salad mix-ins or as a side dish. Leftovers should be stored in the refrigerator inside an air-tight container for 3-5 days.

NUTRITIONS: Calories: 244 Protein: 20.5 g Carbohydrates: 22.5 g Fats: 10 g

MINI MAC IN A BOWL

INGREDIENTS

- 5 ounce of lean ground beef
- Two tablespoons of diced white or yellow onion.
- 1/8 teaspoon of onion powder
- 1/8 teaspoon of white vinegar
- 1 ounce of dill pickle slices
- One teaspoon sesame seed
- 3 cups of shredded Romaine lettuce
- Cooking spray
- Two tablespoons reduced-fat shredded cheddar cheese
- Two tablespoons of Wish-bone light thousand island as dressing

DIRECTIONS

1. Place a lightly greased small skillet on fire to heat,
2. Add your onion to cook for about 2-3 minutes,
3. Next, add the beef and allow cooking until it's brown
4. Next, mix your vinegar and onion powder with the dressing,
5. Finally, top the lettuce with the cooked meat and sprinkle cheese on it, add your pickle slices.
6. Drizzle the mixture with the sauce and sprinkle the sesame seeds also.
7. Your mini mac in a bowl is ready for consumption.

NUTRITIONS: Calories: 150 Protein: 21 g Carbohydrates: 32 gFats: 19 g

LEAN AND GREEN SMOOTHIE 1

INGREDIENTS

- 2 1/2 cups of kale leaves
- 3/4 cup of chilled apple juice
- 1 cup of cubed pineapple
- 1/2 cup of frozen green grapes
- 1/2 cup of chopped apple

DIRECTIONS

1. Place the pineapple, apple juice, apple, frozen seedless grapes, and kale leaves in a blender.
2. Cover and blend until it's smooth.
3. Smoothie is ready and can be garnished with halved grapes if you wish.

NUTRITIONS: Calories: 81 Protein: 2 g Carbohydrates: 19 g Fats: 1 g

LEAN AND GREEN SMOOTHIE 2

INGREDIENTS

- Six kale leaves
- Two peeled oranges
- 2 cups of mango kombucha
- 2 cups of chopped pineapple
- 2 cups of water

DIRECTIONS

1. Break up the oranges, place in the blender,
2. Add the mango kombucha, chopped pineapple, and kale leaves into the blender
3. Blend everything until it is smooth.
4. Smoothie is ready to be taken.

NUTRITIONS: Calories: 81 Protein: 2 g Carbohydrates: 19 g Fats: 1 g

LEAN AND GREEN CHICKEN PESTO PASTA

INGREDIENTS

- 3 cups of raw kale leaves
- 2 tbsp. of olive oil
- 2 cups of fresh basil
- 1/4 teaspoon salt
- 3 tbsp. lemon juice
- Three garlic cloves
- 2 cups of cooked chicken breast
- 1 cup of baby spinach
- 6 ounce of uncooked chicken pasta
- 3 ounces of diced fresh mozzarella
- Basil leaves or red pepper flakes to garnish

DIRECTIONS

1. Start by making the pesto, add the kale, lemon juice, basil, garlic cloves, olive oil, and salt to a blender and blend until its smooth.
2. Add salt and pepper to taste.
3. Cook the pasta and strain off the water. Reserve 1/4 cup of the liquid.
4. Get a bowl and mix everything, the cooked pasta, pesto, diced chicken, spinach, mozzarella, and the reserved pasta liquid.
5. Sprinkle the mixture with additional chopped basil or red paper flakes (optional).
6. Now your salad is ready. You may serve it warm or chilled. Also, it can be taken as a salad mix-ins or as a side dish. Leftovers should be stored in the refrigerator inside an air-tight container for 3-5 days.

NUTRITIONS: Calories: 244 Protein: 20.5 g Carbohydrates: 22.5 g Fats: 10 g

CHAPTER 12.
BREAKFAST 2

ALKALINE BLUEBERRY SPELT PANCAKES

INGREDIENTS

- 2 cups Spelt Flour
- 1 cup Coconut Milk
- 1/2 cup Alkaline Water
- 2 tbsps. Grapeseed Oil
- 1/2 cup Agave
- 1/2 cup Blueberries
- 1/4 tsp. Sea Moss

DIRECTIONS

1. Mix the spelt flour, agave, grapeseed oil, hemp seeds, and the sea moss together in a bowl.
2. Add in 1 cup of hemp milk and alkaline water to the mixture, until you get the consistency mixture you like.
3. Crimp the blueberries into the batter.
4. Heat the skillet to moderate heat then lightly coat it with the grapeseed oil.
5. Pour the batter into the skillet then let them cook for approximately 5 minutes on every side.
6. Serve and Enjoy.

NUTRITIONS: Calories: 203 kcal Fat: 1.4g Carbs: 41.6g Proteins: 4.8g

ALKALINE BLUEBERRY MUFFINS

INGREDIENTS

- 1 cup Coconut Milk
- 3/4 cup Spelt Flour
- 3/4 Teff Flour
- 1/2 cup Blueberries
- 1/3 cup Agave
- 1/4 cup Sea Moss Gel
- 1/2 tsp. Sea Salt
- Grapeseed Oil

DIRECTIONS

1. Adjust the temperature of the oven to 365 degrees.
2. Grease 6 regular-size muffin cups with muffin liners.
3. In a bowl, mix together sea salt, sea moss, agave, coconut milk, and flour gel until they are properly blended.
4. You then crimp in blueberries.
5. Coat the muffin pan lightly with the grapeseed oil.
6. Pour in the muffin batter.
7. Bake for at least 30 minutes until it turns golden brown.
8. Serve.

NUTRITIONS: Calories: 160 kcal Fat: 5g Carbs: 25g Proteins: 2g

CRUNCHY QUINOA MEAL

INGREDIENTS

- 3 cups coconut milk
- 1 cup rinsed quinoa
- 1/8 tsp. ground cinnamon
- 1 cup raspberry
- 1/2 cup chopped coconuts

DIRECTIONS

1. In a saucepan, pour milk and bring to a boil over moderate heat.
2. Add the quinoa to the milk and then bring it to a boil once more.
3. You then let it simmer for at least 15 minutes on medium heat until the milk is reduced.
4. Stir in the cinnamon then mix properly.
5. Cover it then cook for 8 minutes until the milk is completely absorbed.
6. Add the raspberry and cook the meal for 30 seconds.
7. Serve and enjoy.

NUTRITIONS: Calories: 271 kcal Fat: 3.7g Carbs: 54g Proteins: 6.5g

COCONUT PANCAKES

INGREDIENTS

- 1 cup coconut flour
- 2 tbsps. arrowroot powder
- 1 tsp. baking powder
- 1 cup coconut milk
- 3 tbsps. coconut oil

DIRECTIONS

1. In a medium container, mix in all the dry ingredients.
2. Add the coconut milk and 2 tbsps. of the coconut oil then mix properly.
3. In a skillet, melt 1 tsp. of coconut oil.
4. Pour a ladle of the batter into the skillet then swirl the pan to spread the batter evenly into a smooth pancake.
5. Cook it for like 3 minutes on medium heat until it becomes firm.
6. Turn the pancake to the other side then cook it for another 2 minutes until it turns golden brown.
7. Cook the remaining pancakes in the same process.
8. Serve.

NUTRITIONS: Calories: 377 kcal Fat: 14.9g Carbs: 60.7g Protein: 6.4g

QUINOA PORRIDGE

INGREDIENTS

- 2 cups coconut milk
- 1 cup rinsed quinoa
- 1/8 tsp. ground cinnamon
- 1 cup fresh blueberries

DIRECTIONS

1. In a saucepan, boil the coconut milk over high heat.
2. Add the quinoa to the milk then bring the mixture to a boil.
3. You then let it simmer for 15 minutes on medium heat until the milk is reduces.
4. Add the cinnamon then mix it properly in the saucepan.
5. Cover the saucepan and cook for at least 8 minutes until milk is completely absorbed.
6. Add in the blueberries then cook for 30 more seconds.
7. Serve.

NUTRITIONS: Calories: 271 kcal Fat: 3.7g Carbs: 54g Protein: 6.5g

AMARANTH PORRIDGE

INGREDIENTS

- 2 cups coconut milk
- 2 cups alkaline water
- 1 cup amaranth
- 2 tbsps. coconut oil
- 1 tbsp. ground cinnamon

DIRECTIONS

1. In a saucepan, mix in the milk with water then boil the mixture.
2. You stir in the amaranth then reduce the heat to medium.
3. Cook on the medium heat then simmer for at least 30 minutes as you stir it occasionally.
4. Turn off the heat.
5. Add in cinnamon and coconut oil then stir.
6. Serve.

NUTRITIONS: Calories: 434 kcal Fat: 35g Carbs: 27g Protein: 6.7g

BANANA BARLEY PORRIDGE

INGREDIENTS

- 1 cup divided unsweetened coconut milk
- 1 small peeled and sliced banana
- 1/2 cup barley
- 3 drops liquid stevia
- 1/4 cup chopped coconuts

DIRECTIONS

1. In a bowl, properly mix barley with half of the coconut milk and stevia.
2. Cover the mixing bowl then refrigerate for about 6 hours.
3. In a saucepan, mix the barley mixture with coconut milk.
4. Cook for about 5 minutes on moderate heat.
5. Then top it with the chopped coconuts and the banana slices.
6. Serve.

NUTRITIONS: Calories: 159kcal Fat: 8.4g Carbs: 19.8g Proteins: 4.6g

ZUCCHINI MUFFINS

INGREDIENTS

- 1 tbsp. ground flaxseed
- 3 tbsps. alkaline water
- 1/4 cup walnut butter
- 3 medium over-ripe bananas
- 2 small grated zucchinis
- 1/2 cup coconut milk
- 1 tsp. vanilla extract
- 2 cups coconut flour
- 1 tbsp. baking powder
- 1 tsp. cinnamon
- 1/4 tsp. sea salt

DIRECTIONS

1. Tune the temperature of your oven to 375°F.
2. Grease the muffin tray with the cooking spray.
3. In a bowl, mix the flaxseed with water.
4. In a glass bowl, mash the bananas then stir in the remaining ingredients.
5. Properly mix and then divide the mixture into the muffin tray.
6. Bake it for 25 minutes.
7. Serve.

NUTRITIONS: Calories: 127 kcal Fat: 6.6g Carbs: 13g Protein: 0.7g

RECIPES COOKBOOK FOR BEGINNERS

MILLET PORRIDGE

INGREDIENTS

- Sea salt
- 1 tbsp. finely chopped coconuts
- 1/2 cup unsweetened coconut milk
- 1/2 cup rinsed and drained millet
- 1-1/2 cups alkaline water
- 3 drops liquid stevia

DIRECTIONS

1. Sauté the millet in a non-stick skillet for about 3 minutes.
2. Add salt and water then stir.
3. Let the meal boil then reduce the amount of heat.
4. Cook for 15 minutes then add the remaining ingredients. Stir.
5. Cook the meal for 4 extra minutes.
6. Serve the meal with toping of the chopped nuts.

NUTRITIONS: Calories: 219 kcal Fat: 4.5g Carbs: 38.2g Protein: 6.4g

JACKFRUIT VEGETABLE FRY

INGREDIENTS

- 2 finely chopped small onions
- 2 cups finely chopped cherry tomatoes
- 1/8 tsp. ground turmeric
- 1 tbsp. olive oil
- 2 seeded and chopped red bell peppers
- 3 cups seeded and chopped firm jackfruit
- 1/8 tsp. cayenne pepper
- 2 tbsps. chopped fresh basil leaves
- Salt

DIRECTIONS

1. In a greased skillet, sauté the onions and bell peppers for about 5 minutes.
2. Add the tomatoes then stir.
3. Cook for 2 minutes.
4. Then add the jackfruit, cayenne pepper, salt, and turmeric.
5. Cook for about 8 minutes.
6. Garnish the meal with basil leaves.
7. Serve warm.

NUTRITIONS: Calories: 236 kcal Fat: 1.8g Carbs: 48.3g Protein: 7g

ZUCCHINI PANCAKES

INGREDIENTS

- 12 tbsps. alkaline water
- 6 large grated zucchinis
- Sea salt
- 4 tbsps. ground Flax Seeds
- 2 tsps. olive oil
- 2 finely chopped jalapeño peppers
- 1/2 cup finely chopped scallions

DIRECTIONS

1. In a bowl, mix together water and the flax seeds then set it aside.
2. Pour oil in a large non-stick skillet then heat it on medium heat.
3. The add the black pepper, salt, and zucchini.
4. Cook for 3 minutes then transfer the zucchini into a large bowl.
5. Add the flax seed and the scallion's mixture then properly mix it.
6. Preheat a griddle then grease it lightly with the cooking spray.
7. Pour 1/4 of the zucchini mixture into griddle then cook for 3 minutes.
8. Flip the side carefully then cook for 2 more minutes.
9. Repeat the procedure with the remaining mixture in batches.
10. Serve.

NUTRITIONS: Calories: 71 kcal Fat: 2.8g Carbs: 9.8g Protein: 3.7g

SQUASH HASH

INGREDIENTS

- 1 tsp. onion powder
- 1/2 cup finely chopped onion
- 2 cups spaghetti squash
- 1/2 tsp. sea salt

DIRECTIONS

1. Using paper towels, squeeze extra moisture from spaghetti squash.
2. Place the squash into a bowl then add the salt, onion, and the onion powder.
3. Stir properly to mix them.
4. Spray a non-stick cooking skillet with cooking spray then place it over moderate heat.
5. Add the spaghetti squash to pan.
6. Cook the squash for about 5 minutes.
7. Flip the hash browns using a spatula.
8. Cook for 5 minutes until the desired crispness is reached.
9. Serve.

NUTRITIONS: Calories: 44 kcal Fat: 0.6g Carbs: 9.7g Protein: 0.9g

HEMP SEED PORRIDGE

INGREDIENTS

- 3 cups cooked hemp seed
- 1 packet Stevia
- 1 cup coconut milk

DIRECTIONS

1. In a saucepan, mix the rice and the coconut milk over moderate heat for about 5 minutes as you stir it constantly.
2. Remove the pan from the burner then add the Stevia. Stir.
3. Serve in 6 bowls.
4. Enjoy.

NUTRITIONS: Calories: 236 kcal Fat: 1.8g Carbs: 48.3g Protein: 7g

PUMPKIN SPICE QUINOA

INGREDIENTS

- 1 cup cooked quinoa
- 1 cup unsweetened coconut milk
- 1 large mashed banana
- 1/4 cup pumpkin puree
- 1 tsp. pumpkin spice
- 2 tsps. chia seeds

DIRECTIONS

1. In a container, mix all the ingredients.
2. Seal the lid then shake the container properly to mix.
3. Refrigerate overnight.
4. Serve.

NUTRITIONS: Calories: 212 kcal Fat: 11.9g Carbs: 31.7g Protein: 7.3g

CHAPTER 13.
MAINS

BAKED RICOTTA WITH PEARS

INGREDIENTS

- Nonstick cooking spray
- 1 (16-ounce) container whole-milk ricotta cheese
- 2 large eggs
- 1/4 cup white whole-wheat flour or whole-wheat pastry flour
- 1 tablespoon sugar
- 1 teaspoon vanilla extract
- 1/4 teaspoon ground nutmeg
- 1 pear, cored and diced
- 2 tablespoons water
- 1 tablespoon honey

DIRECTIONS

1. Preheat the oven to 400°F. Spray four 6-ounce ramekins with nonstick cooking spray.
2. In a large bowl, beat together the ricotta, eggs, flour, sugar, vanilla, and nutmeg.
3. Spoon into the ramekins.
4. Bake for 22 to 25 minutes, or until the ricotta is just about set.
5. Remove from the oven and cool slightly on racks.
6. While the ricotta is baking, in a small saucepan over medium heat, simmer the pear in the water for 10 minutes, until slightly softened.
7. Remove from the heat, and stir in the honey.
8. Serve the ricotta ramekins topped with the warmed pear.

NUTRITIONS: Calories: 312 Cal Fat: 17g Cholesterol: 163mg Sodium: 130mg Carbohydrates: 23g Fiber: 2g Protein: 17g

PESTO ZUCCHINI NOODLES

INGREDIENTS

- 4 zucchini, spiralized
- 1 tbsp avocado oil
- 2 garlic cloves, chopped
- 2/3 cup olive oil
- 1/3 cup parmesan cheese, grated
- 2 cups fresh basil
- 1/3 cup almonds
- 1/8 tsp. black pepper
- 3/4 tsp. sea salt

DIRECTIONS

1. Add zucchini noodles into a colander and sprinkle with 1/4 teaspoon of salt.
2. Cover and let sit for 30 minutes.
3. Drain zucchini noodles well and pat dry.
4. Preheat the oven to 400 F.
5. Place almonds on a parchment-lined baking sheet and bake for 6-8 minutes.
6. Transfer toasted almonds into the food processor and process until coarse.
7. Add olive oil, cheese, basil, garlic, pepper, and remaining salt in a food processor with almonds and process until pesto texture.
8. Heat avocado oil in a large pan over medium-high heat.
9. Add zucchini noodles and cook for 4-5 minutes.
10. Pour pesto over zucchini noodles, mix well and cook for 1 minute.
11. Serve immediately with baked salmon.

NUTRITIONS: Calories: 525 Cal Fat: 47.4 g Carbohydrates: 9.3 g Sugar: 3.8 g Protein: 16.6 g Cholesterol: 30 mg

STEWED HERBED FRUIT

INGREDIENTS

- 2 cups dried apricots
- 2 cups prunes
- 2 cups dried unsulfured pears
- 2 cups dried apples
- 1 cup dried cranberries
- 1/4 cup honey
- 6 cups water
- 1 teaspoon dried thyme leaves
- 1 teaspoon dried basil leaves

DIRECTIONS

1. In a 6-quart slow cooker, mix all of the ingredients.
2. Cover and cook on low for 6 to 8 hours, or until the fruits have absorbed the liquid and are tender.
3. Store in the refrigerator up to 1 week.
4. You can freeze the fruit in 1-cup portions for more extended storage.

NUTRITIONS: Calories: 242 Cal Carbohydrates: 61 g Sugar: 43 g Fiber: 9 g Fat: 0 g Saturated Fat: 0 g Protein: 2 g Sodium: 11 mg

HERBED WILD RICE

INGREDIENTS

- 3 cups wild rice, rinsed and drained
- 6 cups Roasted Vegetable Broth
- 1 onion, chopped
- 1/2 teaspoon salt
- 1/2 teaspoon dried thyme leaves
- 1/2 teaspoon dried basil leaves
- 1 bay leaf
- 1/3 cup chopped fresh flat-leaf parsley

DIRECTIONS

1. In a 6-quart slow cooker, mix the wild rice, vegetable broth, onion, salt, thyme, basil, and bay leaf.
2. Cover and cook on low for 4 to 6 hours, or until the wild rice is tender but still firm.
3. You can cook this dish longer until the wild rice pops, taking about 7 to 8 hours.
4. Remove and discard the bay leaf.
5. Stir in the parsley and serve.

NUTRITIONS: Calories: 258 Cal Carbohydrates: 54 g Sugar: 3 g Fiber: 5 g Fat: 2 g Saturated Fat: 0 g Protein: 6 g Sodium: 257 mg

BUFFALO CHICKEN SLIDERS

INGREDIENTS

- Chicken breasts (2 lb., cooked, shredded)
- Wing sauce (1 cup)
- Ranch dressing mix (1 pack)
- Blue cheese dressing (1/4 cup, low fat)
- Lettuce (for topping)
- Buns (12, slider)

DIRECTIONS

1. Add the chicken breasts (shredded, cooked) in a large bowl along with the ranch dressing and wing sauce.
2. Stir well to incorporate then place a piece of lettuce onto each slider roll.
3. Top off using chicken mixture.
4. Drizzle blue cheese dressing over chicken then top off using top buns of slider rolls
5. Serve.

NUTRITIONS: Calories: 300 Cal Fat: 14 g Cholesterol: 25 mg

HIGH PROTEIN CHICKEN MEATBALLS

INGREDIENTS

- Chicken (1 lbs., lean, ground)
- Oats (3/4 cup, rolled)
- Onions (2, grated)
- All spice (2 tsp. ground)
- Salt and black pepper (dash)

DIRECTIONS

1. Heat a skillet (large) over medium heat then grease using cooking spray.
2. Add in the onions (grated), chicken (lean, ground), oats (rolled), allspice (earth) and a dash of salt and black pepper in in a large sized bowl, stir well to incorporate.
3. Shape mixture into meatballs (small).
4. Place into the skillet (greased). Cook for roughly 5 minutes until golden brown on all sides.
5. Remove meatballs from heat then serve immediately.

NUTRITIONS: Calories: 519 Cal Protein: 57g Carbohydrates: 32 g Fat :15 g

BARLEY RISOTTO

INGREDIENTS

- 21/4 cups hulled barley, rinsed
- 1 onion, finely chopped
- 4 garlic cloves, minced
- 1 (8-ounce) package button mushrooms, chopped
- 6 cups low-sodium vegetable broth
- 1/2 teaspoon dried marjoram leaves
- 1/8 teaspoon freshly ground black pepper
- 2/3 cup grated Parmesan cheese

DIRECTIONS

1. In a 6-quart slow cooker, mix the barley, onion, garlic, mushrooms, broth, marjoram, and pepper.
2. Cover and cook on low for 7 to 8 hours, or until the barley has absorbed most of the liquid and is tender, and the vegetables are tender.
3. Stir in the Parmesan cheese and serve.

NUTRITIONS: Calories: 288 Cal Carbohydrates: 45 g Sugar: 2 g Fiber: 9 g Fat: 6 g Saturated Fat: 3 g Protein: 13 g Sodium: 495 mg

RISOTTO WITH GREEN BEANS, SWEET POTATOES, AND PEAS

COOKING: 4-5H PREPARATION: 20' SERVES: 8

INGREDIENTS

- 1 large sweet potato, peeled and chopped
- 1 onion, chopped
- 5 garlic cloves, minced
- 2 cups short-grain brown rice
- 1 teaspoon dried thyme leaves
- 7 cups low-sodium vegetable broth
- 2 cups green beans, cut in half crosswise
- 2 cups frozen baby peas
- 3 tablespoons unsalted butter
- 1/2 cup grated Parmesan cheese

DIRECTIONS

1. In a 6-quart slow cooker, mix the sweet potato, onion, garlic, rice, thyme, and broth.
2. Cover and cook on low for 3 to 4 hours, or until the rice is tender.
3. Stir in the green beans and frozen peas.
4. Cover and cook on low for 30 to 40 minutes or until the vegetables are tender.
5. Stir in the butter and cheese. Cover and cook on low for 20 minutes, then stir and serve.

NUTRITIONS: Calories: 385 Cal Carbohydrates: 52 g Sugar: 4 g Fiber: 6 g Fat: 10 g Saturated Fat: 5 g Protein: 10 g Sodium: 426 mg

MAPLE LEMON TEMPEH CUBES

INGREDIENTS

- Tempeh; 1 packet
- Coconut oil; 2 to 3 teaspoons
- Lemon juice; 3 tablespoons
- Maple syrup; 2 teaspoons
- Bragg's Liquid Aminos or low-sodium tamari or (optional); 1 to 2 teaspoons
- Water; 2 teaspoons
- Dried basil; 1/4 teaspoon
- Powdered garlic; 1/4 teaspoon
- Black pepper (freshly grounded); to taste

DIRECTIONS

1. Heat your oven to 400 ° C.
2. Cut your tempeh block into squares in bite form.
3. Heat coconut oil over medium to high heat in a non-stick skillet.
4. When melted and heated, add the tempeh and cook on one side for 2-4 minutes, or until the tempeh turns down into a golden-brown color.
5. Flip the tempeh bits, and cook for 2-4 minutes.
6. Mix the lemon juice, tamari, maple syrup, basil, water, garlic, and black pepper while tempeh is browning.
7. Drop the mixture over tempeh, then swirl to cover the tempeh.
8. Sauté for 2-3 minutes, then turn the tempeh and sauté 1-2 minutes more.
9. The tempeh, on both sides, should be soft and orange.

NUTRITIONS: Carbohydrates: 22 Cal Fats: 17 g Sugar: 5 g Protein: 21 g Fiber: 9 g

BOK CHOY WITH TOFU STIR FRY

INGREDIENTS

- Super-firm tofu; 1 lb. (drained and pressed)
- Coconut oil; one tablespoon
- Clove of garlic; 1 (minced)
- Baby bok choy; 3 heads (chopped)
- Low-sodium vegetable broth;
- Maple syrup; 2 teaspoons
- Braggs liquid aminos
- Sambal oelek; 1 to 2 teaspoons (similar chili sauce)
- Scallion or green onion; 1 (chopped)
- Freshly grated ginger; 1 teaspoon
- Quinoa/rice, for serving

DIRECTIONS

1. With paper towels, Pat pressed the tofu dry and cut into tiny pieces of bite-size around 1/2 inch wide.
2. Heat coconut oil in a wide skillet onto a warm.
3. Remove tofu and stir-fry until painted softly.
4. Stir-fry for 1-2 minutes, before the choy of the Bok, starts to wilt.
5. When this occurs, you'll want to apply the vegetable broth and all the remaining ingredients to the skillet.
6. Hold the mixture stir-frying until all components are well coated, and the bulk of the liquid evaporates, around 5-6 min.
7. Serve over brown rice or quinoa.

NUTRITIONS: Calories: 263.7 Cal Fat 4.2 g Cholesterol: 0.3 mg Sodium: 683.6 mg Potassium: 313.7 mg Carbohydrate: 35.7 g

THREE-BEAN MEDLEY

INGREDIENTS

- 1 1/4 cups dried kidney beans, rinsed and drained
- 1 1/4 cups dried black beans, rinsed and drained
- 1 1/4 cups dried black-eyed peas, rinsed and drained
- 1 onion, chopped
- 1 leek, chopped
- 2 garlic cloves, minced
- 2 carrots, peeled and chopped
- 6 cups low-sodium vegetable broth
- 1 1/2 cups water
- 1/2 teaspoon dried thyme leaves

DIRECTIONS

1. In a 6-quart slow cooker, mix all of the ingredients.
2. Cover and cook on low for 6 to 8 hours, or until the beans are tender and the liquid is absorbed.

NUTRITIONS: Calories: 284 Cal Carbohydrates: 56 g Sugar: 6 g Fiber: 19 g Fat: 0 g Saturated Fat: 0 g Protein: 1 9g Sodium: 131 mg

HERBED GARLIC BLACK BEANS

INGREDIENTS

- 3 cups dried black beans, rinsed and drained
- 2 onions, chopped
- 8 garlic cloves, minced
- 6 cups low-sodium vegetable broth
- 1/2 teaspoon salt
- 1 teaspoon dried basil leaves
- 1/2 teaspoon dried thyme leaves
- 1/2 teaspoon dried oregano leaves

DIRECTIONS

1. In a 6-quart slow cooker, mix all the ingredients.
2. Cover and cook on low for 7 to 9 hours, or until the beans have absorbed the liquid and are tender.
3. Remove and discard the bay leaf

NUTRITIONS: Calories: 250 Cal Carbohydrates: 47 g Sugar: 3 g Fiber: 17 g Fat: 0 g Saturated Fat: 0 g Protein: 15 g Sodium: 253 mg

QUINOA WITH VEGETABLES

INGREDIENTS

- 2 cups quinoa, rinsed and drained
- 2 onions, chopped
- 2 carrots, peeled and sliced
- 1 cup sliced cremini mushrooms
- 3 garlic cloves, minced
- 4 cups low-sodium vegetable broth
- 1/2 teaspoon salt
- 1 teaspoon dried marjoram leaves
- 1/8 teaspoon freshly ground black pepper

DIRECTIONS

1. In a 6-quart slow cooker, mix all of the ingredients.
2. Cover and cook on low for 5 to 6 hours, or until the quinoa and vegetables are tender.
3. Stir the mixture and serve.

NUTRITIONS: Calories: 204 Cal Carbohydrates: 35 g Sugar: 4 g Fiber: 4 g Fat: 3 g Saturated Fat: 0 g Protein: 7 g Sodium: 229 mg

CHAPTER 14.
MAINS 2

BALSAMIC BEEF AND MUSHROOMS MIX

INGREDIENTS

- 2 pounds' beef, cut into strips
- ¼ cup balsamic vinegar
- 2 cups beef stock
- 1 tablespoon ginger, grated
- Juice of ½ lemon
- 1 cup brown mushrooms, sliced
- A pinch of salt and black pepper
- 1 teaspoon ground cinnamon

DIRECTIONS

1. In your slow cooker, mix all the ingredients, cover and cook on low for 8 hours.
2. Divide everything between plates and serve.

NUTRITIONS: Calories: 446 Fat: 14g Fiber: 0.6g Carbs: 2.9 g Protein: 70g

OREGANO PORK MIX

INGREDIENTS

- 2 pounds' pork roast
- 7 ounces' tomato paste
- 1 yellow onion, chopped
- 1 cup beef stock
- 2 tablespoons ground cumin
- 2 tablespoons olive oil
- 2 tablespoons fresh oregano, chopped
- 1 tablespoon garlic, minced
- ½ cup fresh thyme, chopped

DIRECTIONS

1. Heat up a sauté pan with the oil over medium-high heat, add the roast, brown it for 3 minutes on both side and then transfer to your slow cooker.
2. Add the remaining ingredients, toss a bit, cover and cook on low for 7 hours.
3. Slice the roast, divide it between plates and serve.

NUTRITIONS: Calories: 623 Fat: 30.1g Fiber: 6.2g Carbs: 19.3g Protein: 69.2g

SIMPLE BEEF ROAST

INGREDIENTS

- 5 pounds' beef roast
- 2 tablespoons Italian seasoning
- 1 cup beef stock
- 1 tablespoon sweet paprika
- 3 tablespoons olive oil

DIRECTIONS

1. In your slow cooker, mix all the ingredients, cover and cook on low for 8 hours.
2. Carve the roast, divide it between plates and serve.

NUTRITIONS: Calories: 587 Fat: 24.1g Fiber: 0.3g Carbs: 0.9g Protein: 86.5g

CHICKEN BREAST SOUP

INGREDIENTS

- 3 chicken breasts, skinless, boneless, cubed
- 2 celery stalks, chopped
- 2 carrots, chopped
- 2 tablespoons olive oil
- 1 red onion, chopped
- 3 garlic cloves, minced
- 4 cups chicken stock
- 1 tablespoon parsley, chopped

DIRECTIONS

1. In your slow cooker, mix all the ingredients except the parsley, cover and cook on High for 4 hours.
2. Add the parsley, stir, ladle the soup into bowls and serve.

NUTRITIONS: Calories: 387 Fat: 21.2g Fiber: 8.9g Carbs: 26.3g Protein: 25.4g

CAULIFLOWER CURRY

INGREDIENTS

- 1 cauliflower head, florets separated
- 2 carrots, sliced
- 1 red onion, chopped
- ¾ cup coconut milk
- 2 garlic cloves, minced
- 2 tablespoons curry powder
- A pinch of salt and black pepper
- 1 tablespoon red pepper flakes
- 1 teaspoon garam masala

DIRECTIONS

1. In your slow cooker, mix all the ingredients.
2. Cover, cook on high for 5 hours, divide into bowls and serve.

NUTRITIONS: Calories: 160 Fat: 11.5g Fiber: 5.4g Carbs: 14.7g Protein: 3.6g

PORK AND PEPPERS CHILI

INGREDIENTS

- 1 red onion, chopped
- 2 pounds' pork, ground
- 4 garlic cloves, minced
- 2 red bell peppers, chopped
- 1 celery stalk, chopped
- 25 ounces' fresh tomatoes, peeled, crushed
- ¼ cup green chilies, chopped
- 2 tablespoons fresh oregano, chopped
- 2 tablespoons chili powder
- A pinch of salt and black pepper
- A drizzle of olive oil

DIRECTIONS

1. Heat up a sauté pan with the oil over medium-high heat and add the onion, garlic and the meat. Mix and brown for 5 minutes then transfer to your slow cooker.
2. Add the rest of the ingredients, toss, cover and cook on low for 8 hours.
3. Divide everything into bowls and serve.

NUTRITIONS: Calories: 448 Fat: 13g Fiber: 6.6g Carbs: 20.2g Protein: 63g

GREEK STYLE QUESADILLAS

INGREDIENTS

- 4 whole wheat tortillas
- 1 cup Mozzarella cheese, shredded
- 1 cup fresh spinach, chopped
- 2 tablespoon Greek yogurt
- 1 egg, beaten
- ¼ cup green olives, sliced
- 1 tablespoon olive oil
- 1/3 cup fresh cilantro, chopped

DIRECTIONS

1. In the bowl, combine together Mozzarella cheese, spinach, yogurt, egg, olives, and cilantro.
2. Then pour olive oil in the skillet.
3. In the skillet Place one tortilla and spread it with Mozzarella mixture.
4. Top it with the second tortilla and spread it with cheese mixture again.
5. Then place the third tortilla and spread it with all remaining cheese mixture.
6. Cover it with the last tortilla and fry it for 5 minutes from each side over the medium heat.

NUTRITIONS: Calories: 193 Fat: 7.7g Fiber: 3.2g Carbs: 23.6g Protein: 8.3g

LIGHT PAPRIKA MOUSSAKA

INGREDIENTS

- 1 eggplant, trimmed
- 1 cup ground chicken
- 1/3 cup white onion, diced
- 3 oz. Cheddar cheese, shredded
- 1 potato, sliced
- 1 teaspoon olive oil
- 1 teaspoon salt
- ½ cup milk
- 1 tablespoon butter
- 1 tablespoon ground paprika
- 1 tablespoon Italian seasoning
- 1 teaspoon tomato paste

DIRECTIONS

1. Slice the eggplant in length and sprinkle with salt.
2. In the skillet Pour olive oil and add sliced potato.
3. Roast potato for 2 minutes from each side.
4. Then transfer it in the plate.
5. Put eggplant in the skillet and roast it for 2 minutes from each side too.
6. In the pan Pour milk and bring it to boil.
7. Add tomato paste, Italian seasoning, paprika, butter, and Cheddar cheese.
8. Then mix up together onion with ground chicken.
9. Arrange the sliced potato in the casserole in one layer.
10. Then add ½ part of all sliced eggplants.
11. Spread the eggplants with ½ part of chicken mixture.
12. Then add remaining eggplants.
13. Pour the milk mixture over the eggplants.
14. Bake moussaka for 30 minutes at 355F.

NUTRITIONS: Calories: 387 Fat: 21.2g Fiber: 8.9g Carbs: 26.3g Protein: 25.4g

CUCUMBER BOWL WITH SPICES AND GREEK YOGURT

INGREDIENTS

- 4 cucumbers
- ½ teaspoon chili pepper
- ¼ cup fresh parsley, chopped
- ¾ cup fresh dill, chopped
- 2 tablespoons lemon juice
- ½ teaspoon salt
- ½ teaspoon ground black pepper
- ¼ teaspoon sage
- ½ teaspoon dried oregano
- 1/3 cup Greek yogurt

DIRECTIONS

1. Make the cucumber dressing: blend the dill and parsley until you get green mash.
2. Then combine together green mash with lemon juice, salt, ground black pepper, sage, dried oregano, Greek yogurt, and chili pepper.
3. Churn the mixture well.
4. Chop the cucumbers roughly and combine them with cucumber dressing. Mix up well.
5. Refrigerate the cucumber for 20 minutes.

NUTRITIONS: Calories: 114 Fat: 1.6g Fiber: 4.1g Carbs: 23.2g Protein: 7.6g

STUFFED BELL PEPPERS WITH QUINOA

INGREDIENTS

- 2 bell peppers
- 1/3 cup quinoa
- 3 oz. chicken stock
- ¼ cup onion, diced
- ½ teaspoon salt
- ¼ teaspoon tomato paste
- ½ teaspoon dried oregano
- 1/3 cup sour cream
- 1 teaspoon paprika

DIRECTIONS

1. Trim the peppers and remove the seeds.
2. Then combine together chicken stock and quinoa in the pan.
3. Add salt and boil the ingredients for 10 minutes or until quinoa will soak all liquid.
4. Then combine together cooked quinoa with dried oregano, tomato paste, and onion.
5. Fill the bell peppers with the quinoa mixture and arrange in the casserole mold.
6. Add sour cream and bake the peppers for 25 minutes at 365F.
7. Serve the cooked peppers with sour cream sauce from the casserole mold.

NUTRITIONS: Calories: 237 Fat: 10.3 Fiber: 4.5 Carbs: 31.3 Protein: 6.9

MEDITERRANEAN BURRITO

INGREDIENTS

- 2 wheat tortillas
- 2 oz. red kidney beans, canned, drained
- 2 tablespoons hummus
- 2 teaspoons tahini sauce
- 1 cucumber
- 2 lettuce leaves
- 1 tablespoon lime juice
- 1 teaspoon olive oil
- ½ teaspoon dried oregano

DIRECTIONS

1. Mash the red kidney beans until you get a puree.
2. Then spread the wheat tortillas with beans mash from one side.
3. Add hummus and tahini sauce.
4. Cut the cucumber into the wedges and place them over tahini sauce.
5. Then add lettuce leaves.
6. Make the dressing: mix up together olive oil, dried oregano, and lime juice.
7. Drizzle the lettuce leaves with the dressing and wrap the wheat tortillas in the shape of burritos.

NUTRITIONS: Calories: 288 Fat: 10.2 Fiber: 14.6 Carbs: 38.2 Protein: 12.5

SWEET POTATO BACON MASH

INGREDIENTS

- 3 sweet potatoes, peeled
- 4 oz. bacon, chopped
- 1 cup chicken stock
- 1 tablespoon butter
- 1 teaspoon salt
- 2 oz. Parmesan, grated

DIRECTIONS

1. Dice sweet potato and put it in the pan.
2. Add chicken stock and close the lid.
3. Boil the vegetables for until they are soft.
4. After this, drain the chicken stock.
5. Mash the sweet potato with the help of the potato masher. Add grated cheese and butter.
6. Mix up together salt and chopped bacon. Fry the mixture until it is crunchy (10-15 minutes).
7. Add cooked bacon in the mashed sweet potato and mix up with the help of the spoon.
8. It is recommended to serve the meal warm or hot.

NUTRITIONS: Calories: 304 Fat: 18.1 Fiber: 2.9 Carbs: 18.8 Protein: 17

PROSCIUTTO WRAPPED MOZZARELLA BALLS

INGREDIENTS

- 8 Mozzarella balls, cherry size
- 4 oz. bacon, sliced
- ¼ teaspoon ground black pepper
- ¾ teaspoon dried rosemary
- 1 teaspoon butter

DIRECTIONS

1. Sprinkle the sliced bacon with ground black pepper and dried rosemary.
2. Wrap every Mozzarella ball in the sliced bacon and secure them with toothpicks.
3. Melt butter.
4. Brush wrapped Mozzarella balls with butter.
5. Line the baking tray with the parchment and arrange Mozzarella balls in it.
6. Bake the meal for 10 minutes at 365F.

NUTRITIONS: Calories: 323 Fat: 26.8 Fiber: 0.1 Carbs: 0.6 Protein: 20.6

GARLIC CHICKEN BALLS

INGREDIENTS

- 2 cups ground chicken
- 1 teaspoon minced garlic
- 1 teaspoon dried dill
- 1/3 carrot, grated
- 1 egg, beaten
- 1 tablespoon olive oil
- ¼ cup coconut flakes
- ½ teaspoon salt

DIRECTIONS

1. In the mixing bowl mix up together ground chicken, minced garlic, dried dill, carrot, egg, and salt.
2. Stir the chicken mixture with the help of the fingertips until homogeneous.
3. Then make medium balls from the mixture.
4. Coat every chicken ball in coconut flakes.
5. Heat up olive oil in the skillet.
6. Add chicken balls and cook them for 3 minutes from each side. The cooked chicken balls will have a golden-brown color.

NUTRITIONS: Calories: 200 Fat: 11.5 Fiber: 0.6 Carbs: 1.7 Protein: 21.9

CHAPTER 15.
SNACKS RECIPES

VEGGIE FRITTERS

INGREDIENTS

- 2 garlic cloves, minced
- 2 yellow onions, chopped
- 4 scallions, chopped
- 2 carrots, grated
- 2 teaspoons cumin, ground
- ½ teaspoon turmeric powder
- Salt and black pepper to the taste
- ¼ teaspoon coriander, ground
- 2 tablespoons parsley, chopped
- ¼ teaspoon lemon juice
- ½ cup almond flour
- 2 beets, peeled and grated
- 2 eggs, whisked
- ¼ cup tapioca flour
- 3 tablespoons olive oil

DIRECTIONS

1. In a bowl, combine the garlic with the onions, scallions and the rest of the ingredients except the oil, stir well and shape medium fritters out of this mix.
2. Heat oil in a pan over medium-high heat, add the fritters, cook for 5 minutes on each side, arrange on a platter and serve.

NUTRITIONS: Calories 209 Fat 11.2 g Fiber 3 g Carbs 4.4 g Protein 4.8 g

WHITE BEAN DIP

INGREDIENTS

- 15 ounces canned white beans, drained and rinsed
- 6 ounces canned artichoke hearts, drained and quartered
- 4 garlic cloves, minced
- 1 tablespoon basil, chopped
- 2 tablespoons olive oil
- Juice of ½ lemon
- Zest of ½ lemon, grated
- Salt and black pepper to the taste

DIRECTIONS

1. In your food processor, combine the beans with the artichokes and the rest of the ingredients except the oil and pulse well.
2. Add the oil gradually, pulse the mix again, divide into cups and serve as a party dip.

NUTRITIONS: Calories 274 Fat 11.7 g Fiber 6.5 g Carbs 18.5 g Protein 16.5 g

EGGPLANT DIP

INGREDIENTS

- 1 eggplant, poked with a fork
- 2 tablespoons tahini paste
- 2 tablespoons lemon juice
- 2 garlic cloves, minced
- 1 tablespoon olive oil
- Salt and black pepper to the taste
- 1 tablespoon parsley, chopped

DIRECTIONS

1. Put the eggplant in a roasting pan, bake at 400° F for 40 minutes, cool down, peel and transfer to your food processor.
2. Add the rest of the remaining ingredients except the parsley, pulse well, divide into small bowls and serve as an appetizer with the parsley sprinkled on top.

NUTRITIONS: Calories 121 Fat 4.3 g Fiber 1 g Carbs 1.4 g Protein 4.3 g

BULGUR LAMB MEATBALLS

INGREDIENTS

- 1 and ½ cups Greek yogurt
- ½ teaspoon cumin, ground
- 1 cup cucumber, shredded
- ½ teaspoon garlic, minced
- A pinch of salt and black pepper
- 1 cup bulgur
- 2 cups water
- 1 pound lamb, ground
- ¼ cup parsley, chopped
- ¼ cup shallots, chopped
- ½ teaspoon allspice, ground
- ½ teaspoon cinnamon powder
- 1 tablespoon olive oil

DIRECTIONS

1. Combine the bulgur with the water in a bowl, cover the bowl, leave aside for 10 minutes, drain and transfer to a bowl.
2. Add the meat, the yogurt and the rest of the ingredients except the oil, stir well and shape medium meatballs out of this mix.
3. Heat oil in a pan over medium-high heat, add the meatballs, cook them for 7 minutes on each side, arrange them all on a platter and serve as an appetizer.

NUTRITIONS: Calories 300 Fat 9.6 g Fiber 4.6 g Carbs 22.6 g Protein 6.6 g

CUCUMBER BITES

INGREDIENTS

- 1 English cucumber, sliced into 32 rounds
- 10 ounces hummus
- 16 cherry tomatoes, halved
- 1 tablespoon parsley, chopped
- 1 ounce feta cheese, crumbled

DIRECTIONS

1. Spread the hummus on each cucumber round, divide the tomato halves on each, sprinkle the cheese and parsley on to and serve as an appetizer.

NUTRITIONS: Calories 162 Fat 3.4 g Fiber 2 g Carbs 6.4 g Protein 2.4 g

STUFFED AVOCADO

INGREDIENTS

- 1 avocado, halved and pitted
- 10 ounces canned tuna, drained
- 2 tablespoons sun-dried tomatoes, chopped
- 1 and ½ tablespoon basil pesto
- 2 tablespoons black olives, pitted and chopped
- Salt and black pepper to the taste
- 2 teaspoons pine nuts, toasted and chopped
- 1 tablespoon basil, chopped

DIRECTIONS

1. Combine the tuna with the sun-dried tomatoes in a bowl, and the rest of the ingredients except the avocado and stir.
2. Stuff the avocado halves with the tuna mix and serve as an appetizer.

NUTRITIONS: Calories 233 Fat 9 g Fiber 3.5 g Carbs 11.4 g Protein 5.6 g

HUMMUS WITH GROUND LAMB

INGREDIENTS

- 10 ounces hummus
- 12 ounces lamb meat, ground
- ½ cup pomegranate seeds
- ¼ cup parsley, chopped
- 1 tablespoon olive oil
- Pita chips for serving

DIRECTIONS

1. Heat oil in a pan over medium-high heat, add the meat, and brown for 15 minutes stirring often.
2. Spread the hummus on a platter, spread the ground lamb all over, also spread the pomegranate seeds and the parsley and serve with pita chips as a snack.

NUTRITIONS: Calories 133 Fat 9.7 g Fiber 1.7 g Carbs 6.4 g Protein 5 g

WRAPPED PLUMS

INGREDIENTS

- 2 ounces prosciutto, cut into 16 pieces
- 4 plums, quartered
- 1 tablespoon chives, chopped
- A pinch of red pepper flakes, crushed

DIRECTIONS

1. Wrap each plum quarter in a prosciutto slice, arrange them all on a platter, sprinkle the chives and pepper flakes all over and serve.

NUTRITIONS: Calories 30 Fat 1 g Fiber 0 g Carbs 4 g Protein 2 g

CUCUMBER SANDWICH BITES

INGREDIENTS

- 1 cucumber, sliced
- 8 slices whole wheat bread
- 2 tablespoons cream cheese, soft
- 1 tablespoon chives, chopped
- ¼ cup avocado, peeled, pitted and mashed
- 1 teaspoon mustard
- Salt and black pepper to the taste

DIRECTIONS

1. Spread the mashed avocado on each bread slice, also spread the rest of the ingredients except the cucumber slices. Divide the cucumber slices on the bread slices, cut each slice in thirds, arrange on a platter and serve as an appetizer.

NUTRITIONS: Calories 187 Fat 12.4 g Fiber 2.1 g Carbs 4.5 g Protein 8.2 g

CUCUMBER ROLLS

INGREDIENTS

- 1 big cucumber, sliced lengthwise
- 1 tablespoon parsley, chopped
- 8 ounces canned tuna, drained and mashed
- Salt and black pepper to the taste
- 1 teaspoon lime juice

DIRECTIONS

1. Arrange cucumber slices on a working surface, divide the rest of the ingredients, and roll.
2. Arrange all the rolls on a surface and serve as an appetizer.

NUTRITIONS: Calories 200 Fat 6 g Fiber 3.4 g Carbs 7.6 g Protein 3.5 g

OLIVES AND CHEESE STUFFED TOMATOES

INGREDIENTS

- 24 cherry tomatoes, top cut off and insides scooped out
- 2 tablespoons olive oil
- ¼ teaspoon red pepper flakes
- ½ cup feta cheese, crumbled
- 2 tablespoons black olive paste
- ¼ cup mint, torn

DIRECTIONS

1. In a bowl, mix the olives paste with the rest of the ingredients except the cherry tomatoes and whisk well. Stuff the cherry tomatoes with this mix, arrange them all on a platter and serve as an appetizer.

NUTRITIONS: Calories 136 Fat 8.6 g Fiber 4.8 g Carbs 5.6 g Protein 5.1 g

TOMATO SALSA

INGREDIENTS

- 1 garlic clove, minced
- 4 tablespoons olive oil
- 5 tomatoes, cubed
- 1 tablespoon balsamic vinegar
- ¼ cup basil, chopped
- 1 tablespoon parsley, chopped
- 1 tablespoon chives, chopped
- Salt and black pepper to the taste
- Pita chips for serving

DIRECTIONS

1. Mix the tomatoes with the garlic in a bowl, and the rest of the ingredients except the pita chips, stir, divide into small cups and serve with the pita chips on the side.

NUTRITIONS: Calories 160 Fat 13.7 g Fiber 5.5 g Carbs 10.1 g Protein 2.2

CHILI MANGO AND WATERMELON SALSA

INGREDIENTS

- 1 red tomato, chopped
- Salt and black pepper to the taste
- 1 cup watermelon, seedless, peeled and cubed
- 1 red onion, chopped
- 2 mangoes, peeled and chopped
- 2 chili peppers, chopped
- ¼ cup cilantro, chopped
- 3 tablespoons lime juice
- Pita chips for serving

DIRECTIONS

1. In a bowl, mix the tomato with the watermelon, the onion and the rest of the ingredients except the pita chips and toss well. Divide the mix into small cups and serve with pita chips on the side.

NUTRITIONS: Calories 62 Fat g Fiber 1.3 g Carbs 3.9 g Protein 2.3 g

CREAMY SPINACH AND SHALLOTS DIP

INGREDIENTS

- 1 pound spinach, roughly chopped
- 2 shallots, chopped
- 2 tablespoons mint, chopped
- ¾ cup cream cheese, soft
- Salt and black pepper to the taste

DIRECTIONS

1. Combine the spinach with the shallots and the rest of the ingredients in a blender,, and pulse well. Divide into small bowls and serve as a party dip.

NUTRITIONS: Calories 204 Fat 11.5 g Fiber 3.1 g Carbs 4.2 g Protein 5.9 g

FETA ARTICHOKE DIP

INGREDIENTS

- 8 ounces artichoke hearts, drained and quartered
- ¾ cup basil, chopped
- ¾ cup green olives, pitted and chopped
- 1 cup parmesan cheese, grated
- 5 ounces feta cheese, crumbled

DIRECTIONS

1. In your food processor, mix the artichokes with the basil and the rest of the ingredients, pulse well, and transfer to a baking dish.
2. Introduce in the oven, bake at 375° F for 30 minutes and serve as a party dip.

NUTRITIONS: Calories 186 Fat 12.4 g Fiber 0.9 g Carbs 2.6 g Protein 1.5 g

AVOCADO DIP

INGREDIENTS

- ½ cup heavy cream
- 1 green chili pepper, chopped
- Salt and pepper to the taste
- 4 avocados, pitted, peeled and chopped
- 1 cup cilantro, chopped
- ¼ cup lime juice

DIRECTIONS

1. Pour the cream with the avocados and the rest of the ingredients in a blender, and pulse well. Divide the mix into bowls and serve cold as a party dip.

NUTRITIONS: Calories 200 Fat 14.5 g Fiber 3.8 g Carbs 8.1 g Protein 7.6 g

GOAT CHEESE AND CHIVES SPREAD

INGREDIENTS

- 2 ounces goat cheese, crumbled
- ¾ cup sour cream
- 2 tablespoons chives, chopped
- 1 tablespoon lemon juice
- Salt and black pepper to the taste
- 2 tablespoons extra virgin olive oil

DIRECTIONS

1. Mix the goat cheese with the cream and the rest of the ingredients in a bowl, and whisk really well. Keep in the fridge for 10 minutes and serve as a party spread.

NUTRITIONS: Calories 220 Fat 11.5 g Fiber 4.8 g Carbs 8.9 g Protein 5.6 g

CHAPTER 16.
SNACK RECIPES 2

BACON CHEESEBURGER

INGREDIENTS

- 1 lb. lean ground beef
- 1/4 cup chopped yellow onion
- 1 clove garlic, minced
- 1 Tbsp. yellow mustard
- 1 Tbsp. Worcestershire sauce
- 1/2 tsp. salt
- Cooking spray
- 4 ultra-thin slices cheddar cheese, cut into 6 equal-sized rectangular pieces
- 3 pieces of turkey bacon, each cut into 8 evenly-sized rectangular pieces
- 24 dill pickle chips
- 4-6 green leaf lettuce leaves, torn into 24 small square-shaped pieces
- 12 cherry tomatoes, sliced in half

DIRECTIONS

1. Pre-heat oven to 400°F.
2. Combine the garlic, salt, onion, Worcestershire sauce, and beef in a medium-sized bowl, and mix well.
3. Form mixture into 24 small meatballs.
4. Put meatballs onto a foil-lined baking sheet and cook for 12-15 minutes.
5. Leave oven on.
6. Top every meatball with a piece of cheese, then go back to the oven until cheese melts for about 2 to 3 minutes.
7. Let meatballs cool.
8. To assemble bites: on a toothpick layer a cheese-covered meatball, piece of bacon, piece of lettuce, pickle chip, and a tomato half.

NUTRITIONS: Fat: 14 g Cholesterol: 41 mg Carbohydrates: 30 g Protein: 15 g

CHEESEBURGER PIE

INGREDIENTS

- 1 large spaghetti squash
- 1 lb. lean ground beef
- 1/4 cup diced onion
- 2 eggs
- 1/3 cup low-fat, plain Greek yogurt
- 2 Tbsp. Tomato sauce
- 1/2 tsp. Worcestershire sauce
- 2/3 cup reduced-fat, shredded cheddar cheese
- 2 oz. dill pickle slices
- Cooking spray

DIRECTIONS

1. Preheat oven to 400°F. Slice spaghetti squash in half lengthwise; dismiss pulp and seeds.
2. Spray insides with cooking spray.
3. Place squash halves cut-side-down onto a foil-lined baking sheet, and bake for 30 minutes.
4. Once cooked, let cool to before scraping squash flesh with a fork to remove spaghetti-like strands; set aside.
5. Push squash strands in the bottom and up sides of the greased pie pan, creating an even layer.
6. Meanwhile, set up pie filling.
7. In a lightly greased, medium-sized skillet, cook beef and onion over medium heat 8 to 10 minutes, sometimes stirring, until meat is brown.
8. Drain and remove from heat.
9. In a medium-sized bowl, whisk together eggs, tomato paste, Greek yogurt, and Worcestershire sauce. Stir in ground beef mixture.
10. Pour pie filling over squash crust.
11. Sprinkle meat filling with cheese, and then top with dill pickle slices.
12. Bake for 40 minutes.

NUTRITIONS: Calories: 409 Cal Fat: 24.49 g Carbohydrates: 15.06 g Protein: 30.69 g

PERSONAL PIZZA BISCUIT

INGREDIENTS

- 1 sachet OPTAVIA Select
- Buttermilk Cheddar Herb Biscuit
- 2 Tbsp cold water
- Cooking spray
- 2 Tbsp no-sugar-added tomato sauce
- 1/4 cup reduced-fat shredded cheese

DIRECTIONS

1. Preheat oven to 350°F.
2. Mix biscuit and water, and spread mixture into a small, circular crust shape onto a greased, foil-lined baking sheet.
3. Bake for 10 minutes.
4. Top with tomato sauce and cheese, and cook till cheese is melted about 5 minutes.

NUTRITIONS: Fats: 3.2 g Cholesterol: 9.8 m Sodium: 10.5 mg Protein: 3.6 g

CHICKEN AND MUSHROOMS

INGREDIENTS

- 2 Breast of Chicken
- 1 Cup of sliced white champignons
- 1 Cup of sliced green chillies
- 1/2 cup scallions hacked
- 1 Teaspoon of chopped garlic
- 1 cup of low-fat cheddar shredded cheese (1-1,5lb. grams fat / ounce)
- 1 Tablespoon of olive oil
- 1 Tablespoon of butter

DIRECTIONS

1. Fry the chicken breasts with olive oil.
2. When needed, salt and pepper.
3. Grill breasts of chicken in a plate with grill.
4. For every serving weigh 4 ounces of chicken. (Makes 2 servings, leftovers save for another meal).
5. In a butter pan, stir in mushrooms, green peppers, scallions and garlic until smooth, and a little dark.
6. Place the chicken in a baking platter.
7. Cover with mushroom combination.
8. Top on ham.
9. Place the cheese in a 350 * oven until it melts.

NUTRITIONS: Carbohydrates: 2 g Protein: 23 g Fat: 11 g Cholesterol: 112 mg Sodium: 198 mg Potassium: 261 mg

CHICKEN ENCHILADA BAKE

INGREDIENTS

- 5 oz. shredded chicken breast (I boil and shred ahead) or 99 percent fat free White Chicken can be used in a pan.
- 1- Can paste Tomatoes
- 1 – Low sodium chicken broth can be fat free
- 1/4 cup-cheese with low fat mozzarella
- 1 Tablespoon -oil
- 1-tbsp of salt
- Ground cumin, chili powder, garlic powder, oregano and onion powder (all to taste).
- 1 to 2 Zucchini sliced long ways (similar to lasagna noodles) into thin lines.
- Sliced (Optional) olives.

DIRECTIONS

1. Prepare Enchilada Sauce: add olive oil in sauce pan over medium / high heat, stir in tomato paste and seasonings, and heat in chicken broth for 2-3 min.
2. Stirring regularly to boil, turn heat to low for 15 min.
3. Set aside & Cool to ambient temperature.
4. Pull-strip of Zucchini through enchilada sauce and lay flat on the pan's bottom in a small baking pan (88) spray with Pam.
5. Next add the chicken a little less than 1/4 cup of enchilada sauce and mix it.
6. Attach chicken to the covers end to end of the baking tray.
7. Sprinkle over chicken with some bacon.
8. Add another layer of the pulled zucchini via enchilada sauce (similar to lasagna making).
9. When needed, cover with the remaining cheese and olives on top. Bake for 35 to 40 minutes.
10. Keep an eye on them.
11. When the cheese begins burning cover with foil.

NUTRITIONS: Calories: 312 Cal Carbohydrates: 21.3 g Protein: 27 g Fat: 10.2 g

MEDITERRANEAN CHICKEN SALAD

INGREDIENTS

- For Chicken:
- 1 3/4 lb. boneless, skinless chicken breast
- 1/4 teaspoon each of pepper and salt (or as desired)
- 1 1/2 tablespoon of butter, melted
- For Mediterranean Salad:
- 1 cup of sliced cucumber
- 6 cups of romaine lettuce, that is torn or roughly chopped
- 10 pitted Kalamata olives
- 1 pint of cherry tomatoes
- 1/3 cup of reduced-fat feta cheese
- 1/4 teaspoon each of pepper and salt (or lesser)
- 1 small lemon juice (it should be about 2 tablespoons)

DIRECTIONS

1. Preheat your oven or grill to about 350oF.
2. Season the chicken with salt, butter, and black pepper
3. Roast or grill chicken until it reaches an internal temperature of 165oF in about 25 minutes.
4. Once your chicken breasts are cooked, remove and keep aside to rest for about 5 minutes before you slice
5. it.
6. Combine all the salad ingredients you have and toss everything together very well
7. Serve the chicken with Mediterranean salad

NUTRITIONS: Calories: 340 Cal Protein: 45 g Carbohydrates: 9 g Fat: 14 g

JALAPENO LENTIL (CHICKPEA) BURGERS + AVOCADO MANGO PICO

COOKING: 10' **PREPARATION: 15'** **SERVES: 5**

INGREDIENTS

- Dried red lentils; half cup; rinsed
- Chickpeas; 1 to 12 ounces can; rinsed
- Ground cumin; one teaspoon
- Chili powder; one teaspoon
- Sea salt; one teaspoon
- Packed cilantro; half cup
- Garlic cloves minced
- Jalapeno finely chopped
- Red onion; half, small; minced
- Red bell pepper
- Carrot; shredded
- Oat bran/oat flour; 1/4 cup (gluten-free)
- Lettuce/hamburger buns
- For Pico:
- Ripe mango (1) diced
- Ripe avocado (1) diced
- Red onion; half, small; finely diced
- Chopped cilantro; half cup
- Fresh lime juice; half teaspoon
- Sea salt

DIRECTIONS

1. Put all ingredients in a large bowl and mix.
2. Stir in the salt to compare.
3. Put a medium saucepan on medium heat, add lentils plus 1 1/2 cups of water, then bring water to a boil, cover it afterward, lower the heat to low, and then simmer lentils until the water is absorbed.
4. Drain, and set aside some extra water.
5. In a food processor, put the cooked lentils, chickpeas, garlic, sea salt, cilantro, chili powder and cumin, and blend until the beans and lentils are smooth.
6. Add tomato, red pepper, jalapeno, and carrot to compare.
7. Divide into 6 equal parts and use your hands to create dense patties.
8. Heat skillet over a medium-high flame; apply 1/2 tablespoon of olive oil
9. Place a few burgers in at a time and cook on either side for a couple of minutes, just until crisp and golden brown.
10. Repeat with remaining patties and add olive oil whenever desired.
11. Place the patties in a bun or lettuce and finish with mango avocado pico.

NUTRITIONS: Carbohydrates: 34.9 g Calories: 225 Cal Sugar: 7.7 g Fats: 6.1 g

GRANDMA'S RICE

INGREDIENTS

- 40g butter
- 1/2 cup brown sugar
- 1/2 cup arborio rice
- 3 cups milk
- 1/2 tbsp ground cinnamon
- 1/8 tbsp ground nutmeg
- 1 tbsp vanilla paste
- 1/2 cup raisins
- 300ml cream

- 40g butter
- 1/2 cup brown sugar
- 1/2 cup arborio rice
- 3 cups milk
- 1/2 tbsp ground cinnamon
- 1/8 tbsp ground nutmeg
- 1 tbsp vanilla paste
- 1/2 cup raisins
- 300ml cream

DIRECTIONS

1. Preheat oven to 300F.
2. Grease a 1 liter ability oven-evidence dish
3. Heat butter in a saucepan and add sugar and rice.
4. Stir for 1 minute to thoroughly coat rice.
5. Remove from heat and wish in milk, spices, and vanilla.
6. Stir through raisins then pour into prepared dish.
7. Bake for 30 minutes, then remove from the oven and stir well.
8. Drizzle over cream and return to the oven for an additional hour.
9. Check that rice is cooked through.
10. Return to the oven for 15-30 minutes if required.
11. Serve with extra cream and nutmeg.

NUTRITIONS: Fat: 20 g Protein: 23 g Cholesterol: 25 mg Carbohydrates: 30 g Sodium: 1000 mg

BAKED BEEF ZUCCHINI

INGREDIENTS

- 2 large zucchini
- 1 cup minced beef
- 1 cup mushroom, chopped
- 1 tomato, chopped
- 1/2 cup spinach, chopped
- 1 tbsp chives, minced
- 2 tbsp olive oil
- Salt and pepper to taste
- 1 tbsp almond butter
- 1 tsp. garlic powder
- 1 cup cheddar cheese, grated
- 1/3 tsp. ginger powder

DIRECTIONS

1. Preheat the oven to 400 degrees F.
2. Add aluminum foil on a baking sheet.
3. Cut the zucchini in half. Scoop out the seeds and make pockets to stuff it later.
4. In a pan, add the olive oil.
5. Toss the beef until brown.
6. Add the mushroom, tomato, chives, salt, pepper, garlic, ginger, and spinach.
7. Cook for 2 minutes. Take off the heat.
8. Stuff the zucchinis using the mix.
9. Add them onto the baking sheet. Sprinkle the cheese on top.
10. Add the butter on top. Bake for 30 minutes. Serve warm.

NUTRITIONS: Fat: 12.8 g Cholesterol: 79.7 mg Sodium: 615.4 mg Potassium: 925.8 mg Carbohydrate: 26.8 g

BAKED TUNA WITH ASPARAGUS

INGREDIENTS

- 2 tuna steak
- 1 cup asparagus, trimmed
- 1 tsp. almond butter
- 1 tsp. rosemary
- 1/2 tsp. oregano
- 1/2 tsp. garlic powder
- 1tsp lemon juice
- 1/2 tsp. ginger powder
- 1 tbsp olive oil
- 1 tsp. red chili powder
- Salt and pepper to taste

DIRECTIONS

1. Marinate the tuna using oregano, lemon juice, salt, pepper, red chili powder, garlic, ginger, and let it sit for 10 minutes.
2. In a pan, add the olive oil.
3. Fry the tuna steaks 2 minutes per side.
4. In another pan, melt the almond butter.
5. Toss the asparagus with salt, pepper, and rosemary for 3 minutes.
6. Serve.

NUTRITIONS: Fat: 4.7 g Cholesterol: 0.0 mg Sodium: 98.5 mg Potassium: 171.6 mg Carbohydrate: 3.2 g

LAMB STUFFED AVOCADO

INGREDIENTS

- 2 avocados
- 1 1/2 cup minced lamb
- 1/2 cup cheddar cheese, grated
- 1/2 cup parmesan cheese, grated
- 2 tbsp almond, chopped
- 1 tbsp coriander, chopped
- 2 tbsp olive oil
- 1 tomato, chopped
- 1 jalapeno, chopped
- Salt and pepper to taste
- 1 tsp. garlic, chopped
- 1 inch ginger, chopped

DIRECTIONS

1. Cut the avocados in half. Remove the pit and scoop out some flesh to stuff it later.
2. In a skillet, add half of the oil.
3. Toss the ginger, garlic for 1 minute.
4. Add the lamb and toss for 3 minutes.
5. Add the tomato, coriander, parmesan, jalapeno, salt, pepper, and cook for 2 minutes.
6. Take off the heat. Stuff the avocados.
7. Sprinkle the almonds, cheddar cheese, and add olive oil on top.
8. Add to a baking sheet and bake for 30 minutes. Serve.

NUTRITIONS: Fat: 19.5 g Cholesterol: 167.5 mg Sodium: 410.7 mg Potassium: 617.1 mg Carbohydrate: 13.1 g

CHAPTER 17. VEGETABLES

GREEN BEANS

INGREDIENTS

- 1-pound green beans
- ¾-teaspoon garlic powder
- ¾-teaspoon ground black pepper
- 1 ¼-teaspoon salt
- ½-teaspoon paprika

DIRECTIONS

1. Turn on the fryer, insert the basket, grease with olive oil, close the lid, set the fryer at 400 degrees F and preheat for 5 minutes.
2. Meanwhile, put the beans in a bowl, sprinkle generously with olive oil, sprinkle with garlic powder, black pepper, salt and paprika and stir until well coated.
3. Open the air fryer, add the green beans, close with the lid and cook for 8 minutes until golden and crisp, stirring halfway through the frying process.
4. When the fryer beeps, open the lid, transfer the green beans to a serving plate and serve.

NUTRITIONS: Calories: 45 Carbs: 2 g Fat: 11 g Protein: 4 g Fiber: 3 g

ASPARAGUS AVOCADO SOUP

INGREDIENTS

- 1 avocado, peeled, pitted, cubed
- 12 ounces' asparagus
- ½-teaspoon ground black pepper
- 1-teaspoon garlic powder
- 1-teaspoon sea salt
- 2 tablespoons olive oil, divided
- 1/2 of a lemon, juiced
- 2 cups vegetable stock

DIRECTIONS

1. Switch on the air fryer, insert fryer basket, grease it with olive oil, then shut with its lid, set the fryer at 425 degrees F and preheat for 5 minutes.
2. Meanwhile, place asparagus in a shallow dish, drizzle with 1-tablespoon oil, sprinkle with garlic powder, salt, and black pepper and toss until well mixed.
3. Open the fryer, add asparagus in it, close with its lid and cook for 10 minutes until nicely golden and roasted, shaking halfway through the frying.
4. When air fryer beeps, open its lid and transfer asparagus to a food processor.
5. Add remaining ingredients into a food processor and pulse until well combined and smooth.
6. Tip the soup in a saucepan, pour in water if the soup is too thick and heat it over medium-low heat for 5 minutes until thoroughly heated.
7. Ladle soup into bowls and serve.

NUTRITIONS: Calories: 208 Carbs: 2 g Fat: 11 g Protein: 4 g Fiber: 5 g

SWEET POTATO CHIPS

INGREDIENTS

- 2 large sweet potatoes, cut into strips 25 mm thick
- 15 ml of oil
- 10g of salt
- 2g black pepper
- 2g of paprika
- 2g garlic powder
- 2g onion powder

DIRECTIONS

1. Cut the sweet potatoes into strips 25 mm thick.
2. Preheat the air fryer for a few minutes.
3. Add the cut sweet potatoes in a large bowl and mix with the oil until the potatoes are all evenly coated.
4. Sprinkle salt, black pepper, paprika, garlic powder and onion powder. Mix well.
5. Place the French fries in the preheated baskets and cook for 10 minutes at 205°C. Be sure to shake the baskets halfway through cooking.

NUTRITIONS: Calories: 123 Carbs: 2 g Fat: 11 g Protein: 4 g Fiber: 0 g

FRIED ZUCCHINI

INGREDIENTS

- 2 medium zucchinis, cut into strips 19 mm thick
- 60g all-purpose flour
- 12g of salt
- 2g black pepper
- 2 beaten eggs
- 15 ml of milk
- 84g Italian seasoned breadcrumbs
- 25g grated Parmesan cheese
- Nonstick Spray Oil
- Ranch sauce, to serve

DIRECTIONS

1. Cut the zucchini into strips 19 mm thick.
2. Mix with the flour, salt, and pepper on a plate. Mix the eggs and milk in a separate dish. Put breadcrumbs and Parmesan cheese in another dish.
3. Cover each piece of zucchini with flour, then dip them in egg and pass them through the crumbs. Leave aside.
4. Preheat the air fryer, set it to 175°C.
5. Place the covered zucchini in the preheated air fryer and spray with oil spray. Set the timer to 8 minutes and press Start / Pause.
6. Be sure to shake the baskets in the middle of cooking.
7. Serve with tomato sauce or ranch sauce.

NUTRITIONS: Calories: 68 Carbs: 2 g Fat: 11 g Protein: 4 g Fiber: 143g

RECIPES COOKBOOK FOR BEGINNERS

FRIED AVOCADO

INGREDIENTS

- 2 avocados cut into wedges 25 mm thick
- 50g Pan crumbs bread
- 2g garlic powder
- 2g onion powder
- 1g smoked paprika
- 1g cayenne pepper
- Salt and pepper to taste
- 60g all-purpose flour
- 2 eggs, beaten
- Nonstick Spray Oil
- Tomato sauce or ranch sauce, to serve

DIRECTIONS

1. Cut the avocados into 25 mm thick pieces.
2. Combine the crumbs, garlic powder, onion powder, smoked paprika, cayenne pepper and salt in a bowl.
3. Separate each wedge of avocado in the flour, then dip the beaten eggs and stir in the breadcrumb mixture.
4. Preheat the air fryer.
5. Place the avocados in the preheated air fryer baskets, spray with oil spray and cook at 205°C for 10 minutes. Turn the fried avocado halfway through cooking and sprinkle with cooking oil.
6. Serve with tomato sauce or ranch sauce.

NUTRITIONS: Calories: 123 Carbs: 2 g Fat: 11 g Protein: 4 g Fiber: 0 g

VEGETABLES IN AIR FRYER

INGREDIENTS

- 2 potatoes
- 1 zucchini
- 1 onion
- 1 red pepper
- 1 green pepper

DIRECTIONS

1. Cut the potatoes into slices.
2. Cut the onion into rings.
3. Cut the zucchini slices
4. Cut the peppers into strips.
5. Put all the ingredients in the bowl and add a little salt, ground pepper and some extra virgin olive oil.
6. Mix well.
7. Pass to the basket of the air fryer.
8. Select 1600C, 30 minutes.
9. Check that the vegetables are to your liking.
10. Ladle soup into bowls and serve.

NUTRITIONS: Calories: 135 Carbs: 2 g Fat: 11 g Protein: 4 g Fiber: 05g

CRISPY RYE BREAD SNACKS WITH GUACAMOLE AND ANCHOVIES

COOKING: 10'   PREPARATION: 10'   SERVES: 4

INGREDIENTS

- 4 slices of rye bread
- Guacamole
- Anchovies in oil

DIRECTIONS

1. Cut each slice of bread into 3 strips of bread.
2. Place in the basket of the air fryer, without piling up, and we go in batches giving it the touch you want to give it. You can select 180oC, 10 minutes.
3. When you have all the crusty rye bread strips, put a layer of guacamole on top, whether homemade or commercial.
4. In each bread, place 2 anchovies on the guacamole.

NUTRITIONS: Calories: 180 Carbs: 4 g Fat: 11 g Protein: 4 g Fiber: 09 g

MUSHROOMS STUFFED WITH TOMATO

INGREDIENTS

- 8 large mushrooms
- 250g of minced meat
- 4 cloves of garlic
- Extra virgin olive oil
- Salt
- Ground pepper
- Flour, beaten egg and breadcrumbs
- Frying oil
- Fried Tomato Sauce

DIRECTIONS

1. Remove the stem from the mushrooms and chop it. Peel the garlic and chop. Put some extra virgin olive oil in a pan and add the garlic and mushroom stems.
2. Sauté and add the minced meat. Sauté well until the meat is well cooked and season.
3. Fill the mushrooms with the minced meat.
4. Press well and take the freezer for 30 minutes.
5. Pass the mushrooms with flour, beaten egg and breadcrumbs. Beaten egg and breadcrumbs.
6. Place the mushrooms in the basket of the air fryer.
7. Select 20 minutes, 180oC.
8. Distribute the mushrooms once cooked in the dishes.
9. Heat the tomato sauce and cover the stuffed mushrooms.

NUTRITIONS: Calories: 160 Carbs: 2 g Fat: 11 g Protein: 4 g Fiber: 0 g

FENNEL AND ARUGULA SALAD WITH FIG VINAIGRETTE

INGREDIENTS

- 5 Ounces of washed and dried arugula
- 1 small fennel bulb, it can be either shaved or tiny sliced.
- 2 tablespoons of extra virgin oil or any cooking oil
- 1 teaspoon of lemon zest
- 1/2 teaspoon of salt
- Pepper (freshly ground)
- Pecorino

DIRECTIONS

1. Mix the arugula and shaved funnel in a serving bowl.
2. On another bowl, mix the olive oil or cooking oil, lemon zest, salt and pepper
3. Shake together until it becomes creamy and smooth.
4. Pour and dress over the salad, tossing gently for it to combine.
5. Peel or shave out some slices of pecorino and put it on top of the salad
6. Serve immediately

NUTRITIONS: Protein: 2.1 g Carbohydrates: 14.3 g Dietary Fiber: 3.4 g Sugars: 9.1 g Fat: 9.7 g

MIXED POTATO GRATIN

INGREDIENTS

- 6 Yukon Gold potatoes, thinly sliced
- 3 sweet potatoes, peeled and thinly sliced
- 2 onions, thinly sliced
- 4 garlic cloves, minced
- 3 tablespoons whole-wheat flour
- 4 cups 2% milk, divided
- 1 1/2 cups Roasted Vegetable Broth
- 3 tablespoons melted butter
- 1 teaspoon dried thyme leaves
- 1 1/2 cups shredded Havarti cheese

DIRECTIONS

1. Grease a 6-quart slow cooker with straight vegetable oil.
2. In the slow cooker, layer the potatoes, onions, and garlic.
3. In a large bowl, mix the flour with 1/2 cup of the milk until well combined.
4. Gradually add the remaining milk, stirring with a wire whisk to avoid lumps.
5. Stir in the vegetable broth, melted butter, and thyme leaves.
6. Pour the milk mixture over the potatoes in the slow cooker and top with the cheese.
7. Cover and cook on low for 7 to 9 hours, or until the potatoes are tender when pierced with a fork.

NUTRITIONS: Calories: 415 Cal Carbohydrates: 42 g Sugar: 10 g Fiber: 3 g Fat: 22 g Saturated Fat: 13 g Protein: 17 g Sodium: 431 mg

GREEN PEA GUACAMOLE

INGREDIENTS

- 1 teaspoon of crushed garlic
- 1 chopped tomato
- 3 cups of frozen green peas (chopped)
- 5 Green chopped onions
- 1/6 teaspoon of hot sauce
- 1/2 teaspoon of grounded cumin
- 1/2 cup of lime juice

DIRECTIONS

1. Blend the peas, garlic, lime juice and cumin until it is smoothened
2. Stir in the tomatoes, green onion and hot sauce into the mixture
3. Then add salt to taste
4. Cover it and put into the refrigerator for a minimum of 30 minutes.
5. This will allow the flavor to blend very well.

NUTRITIONS: Calories: 40.7 Cal Fat: 0.2 g Cholesterol: 0.0 mg Sodium: 157.4 mg Carbohydrates: 7.6 g Dietary Fiber: 1.7 g Protein: 2.7 g

CHAPTER 18.
VEGETABLES 2

CAULIFLOWER CRUST PIZZA

INGREDIENTS

- 1 cauliflower (it should be cut into smaller portions;
- 1/4 grated parmesan cheese
- 1 egg
- 1 Tsp Italian seasoning
- 1/4 Tsp. kosher salt
- 2 cups of freshly grated mozzarella
- 1/4 cup of spicy pizza sauce.
- Basil leaves, for garnishing.

DIRECTIONS

1. Begin by preheating your oven while using the parchment paper to rim the baking sheet.
2. Process the cauliflower into a fine powder, and then transfer to a bowl, before putting it into the microwave.
3. Leave for about 5-6 minutes to get it soft.
4. Transfer the microwave cauliflower to a clean and dry kitchen towel.
5. Leave it to cool off.
6. When cold, use the kitchen towel to wrap the cauliflower and then get rid of all the moisture by wringing the towel.
7. Continue squeezing until water is gone completely. Put the cauliflower, Italian seasoning, Parmesan, egg, salt, and mozzarella (1 cup).
8. Stir very well until well combined.
9. Transfer the combined mixture to the baking sheet previously prepared, pressing it into a 10-inch round shape. Bake for 10-15 minutes until it becomes golden in color. Take the baked crust out of the oven and use the spicy pizza sauce and mozzarella (the leftover 1 cup) to top it.
10. Bake again for 10 more minutes until the cheese melts and looks bubbly. Garnish using fresh basil leaves. You can also enjoy this with salad.

NUTRITIONS: Calories: 74 Cal Carbohydrates: 4 g Protein: 6 g Fat: 4 g Fiber: 2 g

THAI ROASTED VEGGIES

INGREDIENTS

- 4 large carrots, peeled and cut into chunks
- 2 onions, peeled and sliced
- 6 garlic cloves, peeled and sliced
- 2 parsnips, peeled and sliced
- 2 jalapeño peppers, minced
- 1/2 cup Roasted Vegetable Broth
- 1/3 cup canned coconut milk
- 3 tablespoons lime juice
- 2 tablespoons grated fresh ginger root
- 2 teaspoons curry powder

DIRECTIONS

1. In a 6-quart slow cooker, mix the carrots, onions, garlic, parsnips, and jalapeño peppers.
2. In a small bowl, mix the vegetable broth, coconut milk, lime juice, ginger root, and curry powder until well blended. Pour this mixture into the slow cooker.
3. Cover and cook on low for 6 to 8 hours, do it until the vegetables are tender when pierced with a fork.

NUTRITIONS: Calories: 69 Cal Carbohydrates: 13 g Sugar: 6 g Fiber: 3 g Fat: 3g Saturated Fat: 3g Protein: 1g Sodium: 95mg

ROASTED SQUASH PUREE

INGREDIENTS

- 1 (3-pound) butternut squash, peeled, seeded, and cut into 1-inch pieces
- 3 (1-pound) acorn squash, peeled, seeded, and cut into 1-inch pieces
- 2 onions, chopped
- 3 garlic cloves, minced
- 2 tablespoons olive oil
- 1 teaspoon dried marjoram leaves
- 1/2 teaspoon salt
- 1/8 teaspoon freshly ground black pepper

DIRECTIONS

1. In a 6-quart slow cooker, mix all of the ingredients.
2. Cover and cook on low for 6 to 7 hours, or until the squash is tender when pierced with a fork.
3. Use a potato masher to mash the squash right in the slow cooker.

NUTRITIONS: Calories: 175 Cal Carbohydrates: 38 g Sugar: 1 g Fiber: 3 g Fat: 4 g Saturated Fat: 1 g Protein: 3 g Sodium: 149 mg

CREAMY SPINACH AND MUSHROOM LASAGNA

INGREDIENTS

- 10 lasagna noodles
- 1 package whole milk ricotta
- 2 packages of frozen chopped spinach.
- 4 cups mozzarella cheese (divided and shredded)
- 3/4 cup grated fresh Parmesan
- 3 tablespoons chopped fresh parsley leaves(optional)
- For the Sauce:
- 1/4 cup of butter(unsalted)
- 2 cloves garlic
- 1 pound of thinly sliced cremini mushroom
- 1 diced onion
- 1/4 cup flour
- 4 cups milk, kept at room temperature
- 1 teaspoon basil(dried)
- Pinch of nutmeg
- Salt and freshly ground black pepper, to taste

DIRECTIONS

1. Preheat oven to 352 degrees F.
2. To make the sauce, over a medium portion of heat, melt your butter, Add garlic, mushrooms and onion. Cook and stir at intervals until it becomes tender at about 3-4 minutes.
3. Whisk in flour until lightly browned, it takes about 1 minute for it to become brown.
4. Next, whisk in the milk gradually, and cook, whisking always, about 2-3 minute till it becomes thickened. Stir in basil, oregano and nutmeg, season with salt and pepper for taste;
5. Then set aside.
6. In another pot of boiling salted water, cook lasagna noodles according to the package instructions.
7. Spread 1 cup mushroom sauce onto the bottom of a baking dish; top it with 4 lasagna noodles, 1/2 of the spinach, 1 cup mozzarella cheese and 1/4 cup Parmesan.
8. Repeat this process with remaining noodles, mushroom sauce and cheeses.
9. Place into oven and bake for 35-45 minutes, or until it starts bubbling. Then boil for 2-3 minutes until it becomes brown and translucent.
10. Let cool 15 minutes.
11. Serve it with garnished parsley (Optional)

NUTRITIONS: Calories: 488.3 Cal Fats: 19.3 g Cholesterol: 88.4 mg Sodium: 451.9 mg Carbohydrates: 51.0 g Dietary Fiber: 7.0 g Protein: 25.0 g

KALE SLAW AND STRAWBERRY SALAD + POPPYSEED DRESSING

COOKING: 20' PREPARATION: 10' SERVES: 2

INGREDIENTS

- Chicken breast; 8 ounces; sliced and baked
- Kale; 1 cup; chopped
- Slaw mix; 1 cup (cabbage, broccoli slaw, carrots mixed)
- Slivered almonds; 1/4 cup
- Strawberries; 1 cup; sliced
- For the dressing:
- Light mayonnaise; 1 tablespoon
- Dijon mustard
- Olive oil; 1 tablespoon
- Apple cider vinegar; 1 tablespoon
- Lemon juice; 1/2 teaspoon
- 1 tablespoon of Honey
- Onion powder; 1/4 teaspoon
- Garlic powder; 1/4 teaspoon
- Poppyseeds

DIRECTIONS

1. Whisk the dressing ingredients together until well mixed, then leave to cool in the fridge.
2. Slice the chicken breasts.
3. Divide 2 bowls of spinach, slaw, and strawberries.
4. Cover with a sliced breast of chicken (4 oz. each), then scatter with almonds.
5. Divide the salad over the dressing and drizzle.

NUTRITIONS: Calories: 340 Cal Fats: 13.6 g Saturated Fat: 6.2 g

ROASTED ROOT VEGETABLES

INGREDIENTS

- 6 carrots, cut into 1-inch chunks
- 2 yellow onions, each cut into 8 wedges
- 2 sweet potatoes, peeled and cut into chunks
- 6 Yukon Gold potatoes, cut into chunks
- 8 whole garlic cloves, peeled
- 4 parsnips, peeled and cut into chunks
- 3 tablespoons olive oil
- 1 teaspoon dried thyme leaves
- 1/2 teaspoon salt
- 1/8 teaspoon freshly ground black pepper

DIRECTIONS

1. In a 6-quart slow cooker, mix all of the ingredients.
2. Cover and cook on low for 6 to 8 hours, or until the vegetables are tender.

NUTRITIONS: Calories: 214 Cal Carbohydrates: 40 g Sugar: 7 g Fiber: 6 g Fat: 5 g Saturated Fat: 1 g Protein: 4 g Sodium: 201 mg

HUMMUS

COOKING: 10' PREPARATION: 10' SERVES: 32

INGREDIENTS

- 4 cups of cooked garbanzo beans
- 1 cup of water
- 1 1/2 tablespoons of lemon juice
- 2 teaspoons of ground cumin • 1 1/2 teaspoon of ground coriander.
- 1 teaspoon of finely chopped garlic
- 1/2 teaspoon of salt
- 1/4 teaspoon of fresh ground pepper
- Paprika for garnish.

DIRECTIONS

1. On a food processor, place together the garbanzo beans, lemon juice, water, garlic, salt and pepper and process it until it becomes smooth and creamy.
2. To achieve your desired consistency, add more water.
3. Then spoon out the hummus in a serving bowl
4. Sprinkle your paprika and serve.

NUTRITIONS: Protein: 0.7 g Carbohydrates: 2.5 g Dietary Fiber: 0.6 g Sugars: 0 g Fat: 1.7 g

CRISPY-TOPPED BAKED VEGETABLES

INGREDIENTS

- 2 tbsp olive oil
- 1 onion, chopped
- 1 celery stalk, chopped
- 2 carrots, grated
- 1/2-pound turnips, sliced
- 1 cup vegetable broth
- 1 tsp. turmeric
- Sea salt and black pepper, to taste
- 1/2 tsp. liquid smoke
- 1 cup Parmesan cheese, shredded
- 2 tbsp fresh chives, chopped

DIRECTIONS

1. Set oven to 360°F and grease a baking dish with olive oil.
2. Set a skillet over medium heat and warm olive oil.
3. Sweat the onion until soft, and place in the turnips, carrots and celery; and cook for 4 minutes.
4. Remove the vegetable mixture to the baking dish.
5. Combine vegetable broth with turmeric, pepper, liquid smoke, and salt.
6. Spread this mixture over the vegetables.
7. Sprinkle with Parmesan cheese and bake for about 30 minutes.
8. Garnish with chives to serve.

NUTRITIONS: Calories: 242 Cal Fats: 16.3 g Carbohydrates: 8.6 g Protein: 16.3 g

VEGAN EDAMAME QUINOA COLLARD WRAPS

INGREDIENTS

- For the wrap:
- Collard leaves; 2 to 3
- Grated carrot; 1/4 cup
- Sliced cucumber; 1/4 cup
- Red bell pepper; 1/4; thin strips
- Orange bell pepper; 1/4; thin strips
- Cooked quinoa; 1/3 cup
- Shelled defrosted edamame; 1/3 cup
- For the dressing:
- Fresh ginger root; 3 tablespoons; peeled + chopped
- Cooked chickpeas; 1 cup
- Clove of garlic; 1
- Rice vinegar; 4 tablespoons
- Low sodium tamari/coconut aminos; 2 tablespoons
- Lime juice; 2 tablespoons
- Water; 1/4 cup
- Few pinches of chili flakes
- Stevia; 1 pack

DIRECTIONS

1. For the dressing, combine all the ingredients and purée in a food processor until smooth.
2. Load into a little jar or tub, and set aside.
3. Place the collar leaves on a flat surface, covering one another to create a tighter tie.
4. Take 1 tablespoon of ginger dressing and blend it up with the prepared quinoa.
5. Spoon the prepared quinoa onto the leaves and shape a simple horizontal line at the closest end.
6. Supplement with the edamame with all the veggie fillings left over.
7. Drizzle around 1 tablespoon of the ginger dressing on top, then fold the cover's sides inwards.
8. Pullover the fillings the side of the cover closest to you, then turn the whole body away to seal it up.

NUTRITIONS: Calories: 295 Cal Sugar: 3 g Sodium: 200 mg Fat: 13 g

GRILLED EGGPLANTS

INGREDIENTS

- 1 large eggplant, cut into thick circles
- Salt and pepper to taste
- 1 tsp. smoked paprika
- 1 tbsp coconut flour
- 1 tsp. lime juice
- 1 tbsp olive oil

DIRECTIONS

1. Coat the eggplants in smoked paprika, salt, pepper, lime juice, coconut flour, and let it sit for 10 minutes.
2. In a grilling pan, add the olive oil.
3. Grill the eggplants for 3 minutes on each side.
4. Serve.

NUTRITIONS: Fat: 0.1 g Sodium: 1.6 mg Carbohydrates: 4.8 g Fiber: 2.4 g Sugars: 2.9 g Protein: 0.8 g

CHAPTER 19. MEAT

TOMATILLO AND GREEN CHILI PORK STEW

INGREDIENTS

- 2 scallions, chopped
- 2 cloves of garlic
- 1 lb. tomatillos, trimmed and chopped
- 8 large romaine or green lettuce leaves, divided
- 2 Serrano chilies, seeds, and membranes
- 1/2 tsp. of dried Mexican oregano (or you can use regular oregano)
- 1 1/2 lb. of boneless pork loin, to be cut into bite-sized cubes
- 1/4 cup of cilantro, chopped
- 1/4 tablespoon (each) salt and paper
- 1 jalapeno, seeds and membranes to be removed and thinly sliced
- 1 cup of sliced radishes
- 4 lime wedges

DIRECTIONS

1. Combine scallions, garlic, tomatillos, 4 lettuce leaves, Serrano chilies, and oregano in a blender.
2. Then puree until smooth.
3. Put pork and tomatillo mixture in a medium pot. 1-inch of puree should cover the pork; if not, add water until it covers it.
4. Season with pepper & salt, and cover it simmers.
5. Simmer on low heat for approximately 20 minutes.
6. Now, finely shred the remaining lettuce leaves.
7. When the stew is done cooking, garnish with cilantro, radishes, finely shredded lettuce, sliced jalapenos, and lime wedges.

NUTRITIONS: Calories: 370 Cal Proteins: 36 g Carbohydrates: 14 g Fat: 19 g

TOMATO BRAISED CAULIFLOWER WITH CHICKEN

INGREDIENTS

- 4 garlic cloves, sliced
- 3 scallions, to be trimmed and cut into 1-inch pieces
- 1/4 teaspoon of dried oregano
- 1/4 teaspoon of crushed red pepper flakes
- 4 1/2 cups of cauliflower
- 1 1/2 cups of diced canned tomatoes
- 1 cup of fresh basil, gently torn
- 1/2 teaspoon each of pepper and salt, divided
- 1 1/2 teaspoon of olive oil
- 1 1/2 lb. of boneless, skinless chicken breasts

DIRECTIONS

1. Get a saucepan and combine the garlic, scallions, oregano, crushed red pepper, cauliflower, tomato, and add 1/4 cup of water.
2. Get everything boil together, add 1/4 teaspoon of pepper and salt for seasoning, and then cover the pot with a lid.
3. Let it simmer for 10 minutes and stir as often as possible until you observe that the cauliflower is tender.
4. Now, wrap up the seasoning with the remaining 1/4 teaspoon of pepper and salt.
5. Toss the chicken breast with olive oil and let it roast in the oven with the heat of 450ºF for 20 minutes and an internal temperature of 165ºF.
6. Allow the chicken to rest for like 10 minutes.
7. Now slice the chicken, and serve on a bed of tomato braised cauliflower.

NUTRITIONS: Calories 290 Cal Fat: 10 g Carbohydrates: 15 g Protein: 38 g

GRILLED CHICKEN POWER BOWL WITH GREEN GODDESS DRESSING

COOKING: 45'   PREPARATION: 5'   SERVES: 4

INGREDIENTS

- 1 1/2 boneless, skinless chicken breasts
- 1/4 tsp. each salt & pepper
- 1 cup rice or cubed kabocha squash
- 1 cup diced zucchini
- 1 cup rice yellow summer squash
- 1 cup rice broccoli
- 8 cherry tomatoes, halved
- 4 radishes, sliced thin
- 1 cup shredded red cabbage
- 1/4 cup hemp or pumpkin seeds
- Green Goddess Dressing
- 1/2 cup low-fat plain Greek yogurt
- 1 cup fresh basil
- 1 clove garlic
- 4 tbsp lemon juice
- 1/4 tsp. each salt & pepper

DIRECTIONS

1. Pre-heat oven to 350°F. Season chicken with salt and pepper.
2. Roast chicken about 10-12 minutes until it reaches a temperature of 165°F.
3. When done, dismiss from oven and set aside to rest, about 5 minutes.
4. Cut into bite-sized pieces and keep warm.
5. While the chicken rests, steam riced kabocha squash, yellow summer squash, zucchini, and broccoli in a covered microwave-proof bowl about 5 minutes till tender.
6. For the dressing, arrange the ingredients in a blender and puree till smooth.
7. To serve, put an equal amount of the riced veggie mixture into four individual serving bowls.
8. Add an equal amount of cherry tomatoes, radishes, and shredded cabbage to each bowl along with a quarter of the chicken and one tablespoon of seeds.
9. Drizzle dressing on top.

NUTRITIONS: Calories: 300 Cal Protein: 43 g Carbohydrates: 12 g Fat: 10 g

CUMIN-LIME STEAK

INGREDIENTS

- Seaweed
- 20 Once. Steak with lean rib-eye
- 6 Tops of Broccoli
- 1 Pack of quick bovine soup (prepared as directed) or 1/2 cup of beef broth
- 1/4 tablespoon lime juice
- 1 1/2 spoonful of ground cumin
- 1 1/2 spoonful of ground coriander
- 2 Big, finely chopped cloves of garlic
- 3 Pounds of olive oil

DIRECTIONS

1. Mix all marinade ingredients (except oil) together in a blender.
2. Add oil to mixer with motor working slowly.
3. Refrigerate and cover until ready to use. Pour 1 cup of marinade over steaks in a glass dish, covering with all sides.
4. Cover and leave to cool for 6 hours (or overnight).
5. Grill over medium-sized coals, turning regularly and clean with 1/2 cup marinade left over.
6. Steam broccoli on the side and serve.

NUTRITIONS: Fats: 0.7 g Sodium: 6.1 mg Carbohydrates: 4.5 g

CHICKEN STRIPS

INGREDIENTS

- 1 Medifast Snack Cracker Pack
- 6 Ounces breast, cut into strips
- 2 Pockets. Walden Farms Dressing Salad, every taste

DIRECTIONS

1. Preheat oven to 350 ° C. Pulse 1 packet of Medifast Snack Crackers in a food processor.
2. These must be pulsed into excellent crumbs.
3. Dip chicken SEED gently into dressing for Walden Farms Salad.
4. Shake off overdressing.
5. In essence, you just want to get the chicken wet so that the crumbs can stick to them.
6. Press the strips of chicken over the crumbs.
7. Take your time and get sweet, coated chicken.
8. Then spray Pam or some other non-stick cooking spray to a baking sheet.
9. Place the chicken on the sheet and bake within 30-40 minutes.

NUTRITIONS: Fat: 25.7 g Fiber: 2.2 g Protein: 35.4 g

CHICKEN STIR FRY

INGREDIENTS

- Boneless and skinless breast of chicken
- I cup each of chopped red bell paper and green bell pepper
- 1 cup of broccoli slaw
- I teaspoon of crushed red pepper
- 1/2 cup of chicken broth
- 2 tablespoon soy sauce

DIRECTIONS

1. Add chopped red and green bell pepper into the chicken broth, add the broccoli slaw also.
2. Next, add your soy sauce, red pepper, and the boneless chicken (shredded).
3. Stir and allow to cook for a few minutes, do this until the peppers are tender and your delicacy is ready.

NUTRITIONS: Calories 137.0 Cal Fats 1.2 g Cholesterol: 27.5 mg Sodium: 873.4 mg Total Carbs: 15.4 g Dietary Fiber: 7.0 g Protein: 15.1 g

TURKEY TACO

INGREDIENTS

- 2 pre-made rolls (1/3 lean, 1 1/3 condiment)
- 4 ounces of turkey (2/3 thin) white meat leftover from Thanksgiving!
- 2 Tablespoons of salad with cranberry (1/4 snack, 1/8th green)
- Shredded laitoux

DIRECTIONS

1. Toast the buns with 2.
2. Next put 1 tablespoon of sugar-free cranberry salad, then 2 ounces of turkey and top with a little shredded lettuce.
3. Fold up like a taco, and eat. 2 Tacos is equivalent to 1 serving.
4. 1 Lean, 1/3 seasoning, 1/4 snack, 1/8 orange.
5. You will need to combine this with a green to make it a lean and nutritious meal in its entirety.

NUTRITIONS: Protein: 17.6 g Carbohydrates: 4.8 g Fats: 7.2 g Cholesterol: 62.7 mg

BRAISED COLLARD GREENS IN PEANUT SAUCE WITH PORK TENDERLOIN

COOKING: 60' **PREPARATION: 10'** **SERVES: 4**

INGREDIENTS

- 2 cups of chicken stock
- 12 cups of chopped collard greens
- 5 tablespoon of powdered peanut butter
- 3 cloves of garlic, crushed
- 1 teaspoon of salt
- 1/2 teaspoon of allspice
- 1/2 teaspoon of black pepper
- 2 teaspoon of lemon juice
- 3/4 teaspoon of hot sauce
- 1 1/2 lb. of pork tenderloin

DIRECTIONS

1. Get a pot with a tight-fitting lid and combine the collards with the garlic, chicken stock, hot sauce, and half of the pepper and salt.
2. Cook on low heat for about 1 hour or until the collards become tender.
3. Once the collards are tender, stir in the allspice, lemon juice.
4. And powdered peanut butter.
5. Keep warm.
6. Season the pork tenderloin with the remaining pepper and salt, and broil in a toaster oven for 10 minutes when you have an internal temperature of 145oF.
7. Make sure to turn the tenderloin every 2 minutes to achieve an even browning all over.
8. After that, you can take away the pork from the oven and allow it to rest for like 5 minutes.
9. Slice the pork as you will like and serve it on top of the braised greens.

NUTRITIONS: Calories: 320 Cal Fat: 10 g Carbohydrates: 15 g Protein: 45 g

TURKEY CAPRESE MEATLOAF CUPS

INGREDIENTS

- 1 large egg
- 2 pounds ground turkey breast
- 3 pieces of sun-dried tomatoes,
- drained and chopped
- 1/4 cup fresh basil leaves,
- chopped
- 5 ounces low-fat fresh mozzarella, shredded
- 1/2 teaspoon garlic powder
- 1/4 teaspoon salt and 1/2 teaspoon pepper, to taste

DIRECTIONS

1. Preheat oven to 400°F.
2. Beat the egg in a big mixing bowl.
3. Add the remaining ingredients and mix everything with your hands until evenly combined.
4. Spray a 12-cup muffin tin and divide the turkey mixture among the muffin cups, pressing the mix in.
5. Cook in the preheated oven till the turkey is well-cooked for about 25-30 minutes.
6. Chill the meatloaves entirely and store them in a container in the fridge for up to 5 days.

NUTRITIONS: Fats: 14 g Cholesterol: 87.1 g Sodium: 174. 4 g Potassium: 73.9 g Carbohydrates: 1.4 g Protein: 16.9 g

MEDITERRANEAN GRILLED CHICKEN

INGREDIENTS

- 2 tbsp. of olive oil
- 3 spoonfuls of white cider vinegar
- 1 Italian Seasoning Teaspoon
- 1 A garlic clove
- 1/4 cubic teaspoon black pepper
- One half lemon zest
- 1 Tablespoon of sun-dried, diced tomatoes
- Excellent for salt and pepper
- 14 Once. Non skinless chicken breast
- Summer squash: 3/4 cup
- 3/4 Cup Cockroach
- Oregano (with option)

DIRECTIONS

1. Combine all ingredients (except chicken) into a large plastic bag with a zip-top.
2. Add marinade to chicken, seal bag and coat meat.
3. For extra flavor, cool down for 30 minutes or longer.
4. Remove from marinade chicken, and discard marinade.
5. Grill the chicken for 6-7 minutes per side over medium heat or until cooked.
6. Place the zucchini and squash on grill (if necessary, on top of the foil).
7. Sprinkle with the flour, oregano and pepper.
8. Switch to cooking thoroughly once.

NUTRITIONS: Carbohydrates: 7 g Protein: 33 g Fat: 23 g Cholesterol: 97 mg Sodium: 301 mg Potassium: 762 mg

AVOCADO CHICKEN SALAD

INGREDIENTS

- 10 oz. diced cooked chicken
- 1/2 cup 2% Plain Greek yogurt
- 3 oz. chopped avocado
- 12 tsp. garlic powder
- 1/4 tsp. salt
- 1/8 tsp. pepper
- 1 tbsp + 1 tsp. lime juice
- 1/4 cup fresh cilantro, chopped

DIRECTIONS

1. Combine all ingredients in a medium-sized bowl.
2. Refrigerate until ready to serve.
3. Cut the chicken salad in half and serve with your favorite greens.

NUTRITIONS: Calories: 242 Cal Fats: 13 g Cholesterol: 44 mg Sodium: 553 mg Potassium: 581 mg Carbohydrates: 18 g

CHICKEN CRUST MARGHERITA PIZZA

INGREDIENTS

- 1/2 lb. ground chicken
- breast
- 1 egg
- 2 Tbsp grated parmesan
- cheese
- 1/2 tsp. Italian seasoning
- Cooking spray
- 1/2 cup no-sugar-added tomato sauce
- 1/2 cup reduced-fat shredded mozzarella cheese
- 2 plum tomatoes, sliced
- 1/4 cup chopped basil

DIRECTIONS

1. Preheat oven to 400 °F.
2. Arrange the first 4 ingredients in a medium-sized bowl.
3. Form the chicken mixture into a circular crust shape onto a parchment-lined, lightly greased baking sheet. Bake until golden, about 20 minutes.
4. Add cheese, sauce and tomato slice, and cook till cheese is melted about 10 minutes.
5. Finally, add fresh basil before serving.
6. After that, you can take away the pork from the oven and allow it to rest for like 5 minutes.
7. Slice the pork as you will like and serve it on top of the braised greens.

NUTRITIONS: Carbohydrates: 0.49 g Fats: 4.61 g Cholesterol: 33 mg Sodium: 138 mg Protein: 11.14 g

CHAPTER 20.
SOUPS AND STEWS

ROASTED TOMATO SOUP

INGREDIENTS

- 3 pounds of tomatoes in a halved manner
- 6 garlic(smashed)
- 2 onions (cut)
- 4 teaspoon of cooking oil or virgin oil
- Salt to taste
- Fresh grinded pepper • 1/4 cup of heavy cream(optional)
- Sliced fresh basil leaves for garnish

DIRECTIONS

1. Oven medium heat of about 427f, preheat the oven.
2. In your mixing bowl, mix the halved tomatoes, garlic, olive oil, onions, salt and pepper
3. Spread the tomato mixture on already prepared baking sheet
4. For a process of 20- 28 minutes, roast and stir
5. Then remove it from the oven and the roasted vegetables should now be transferred to a soup pot
6. Stir in the basil leaves
7. Blend in small portions in a blender
8. Serve immediately

NUTRITIONS: Fat: 5.9 g Cholesterol: 0 mg Sodium: 26 mg Potassium: 590.7 mg Carbohydrate: 12.6 g Protein: 2.3 g

CHEESEBURGER SOUP

INGREDIENTS

- 1/4 cup of chopped onion
- 1 quantity of 14.5 oz. can diced tomato
- 1 lb. of 90% lean ground beef
- 3/4 cup of chopped celery
- 2 teaspoon of Worcestershire sauce
- 3 cups of low sodium chicken broth
- 1/4 teaspoon of salt
- 1 teaspoon of dried parsley
- 7 cups of baby spinach
- 1/4 teaspoon of ground pepper
- 4 oz. of reduced-fat shredded cheddar cheese

DIRECTIONS

1. Get a large soup pot and cook the beef until it becomes brown.
2. Add the celery, onion, and sauté until it becomes tender.
3. Remove from the heat and drain excess liquid. Stir in the broth, tomatoes, parsley, Worcestershire sauce, pepper, and salt.
4. Cover with the lid and allow it to simmer on low heat for about 20 minutes.
5. Add spinach and leave it to cook until it becomes wilted in about 1-3 minutes.
6. Top each of your servings with 1 ounce of cheese.

NUTRITIONS: Calories: 400 Cal Carbohydrates: 11 g Protein: 44 gFat: 20 g

QUICK LENTIL CHILI

INGREDIENTS

- 11/2 cups of seeded or diced pepper
- 11/2 cups of coarsely chopped onions 5 cups of vegetable broth (it should have a low sodium content)
- 1 tablespoon of garlic
- 1/4 teaspoon of freshly ground pepper
- 1 cup of red lentils
- 3 filled teaspoons of chili powder
- 1 tablespoon of grounded cumin

DIRECTIONS

1. Place your pot over medium heat
2. Combine your onions, red peppers, low sodium vegetable broth, garlic, salt and pepper
3. Cook and stir always until the onions are more translucent and all the liquid evaporated. This will take about 10mins.
4. Add the remaining broth, lime juice, chili powder, lentils, cumin and boil.
5. Reduce heat at this point, cover it for about 15minutes to shimmer until the lentils are appropriately cooked
6. Add a little water if the mixture seems to be thick.
7. The chili will be appropriately done when most of the water is absorbed.
8. Serve and enjoy.

NUTRITIONS: Protein: 2.3 g Carbohydrates: 12.1 g Dietary Fiber: 3.3 g Sugars: 6.1 g Fat: 2.9 g

LEMON GARLIC OREGANO CHICKEN WITH ASPARAGUS

INGREDIENTS

- 1 small lemon, juiced (this should be about 2 tablespoons of lemon juice)
- 1 3/4 lb. of bone-in, skinless chicken thighs
- 2 tablespoon of fresh oregano, minced
- 2 cloves of garlic, minced
- 2 lbs. of asparagus, trimmed
- 1/4 teaspoon each or less for black pepper and salt

DIRECTIONS

1. Preheat the oven to about 350oF. Put the chicken in a medium-sized bowl.
2. Now, add the garlic, oregano, lemon juice, pepper, and salt and toss together to combine.
3. Roast the chicken in the oven until it reaches an internal temperature of 165oF in about 40 minutes.
4. Once the chicken thighs have been cooked, remove and keep aside to rest.
5. Now, steam the asparagus on a stovetop or in a microwave to the desired doneness.
6. Serve asparagus with the roasted chicken thighs.

NUTRITIONS: Calories: 350 Cal Fat: 10 g Carbohydrates: 10 g Protein: 32 g

CREAMY CAULIFLOWER SOUP

INGREDIENTS

- 5 cups cauliflower rice
- 8 oz. cheddar cheese, grated
- 2 cups unsweetened almond milk
- 2 cups vegetable stock
- 2 tbsp water
- 1 small onion, chopped
- 2 garlic cloves, minced
- 1 tbsp olive oil
- Pepper
- Salt

DIRECTIONS

1. Heat olive oil in a large stockpot over medium heat.
2. Add onion and garlic and cook for 1-2 minutes. Add cauliflower rice and water.
3. Cover and cook for 5-7 minutes.
4. Now add vegetable stock and almond milk and stir well.
5. Bring to boil.
6. Turn heat to low and simmer for 5 minutes.
7. Turn off the heat.
8. Slowly add cheddar cheese and stir until smooth.
9. Season soup with pepper and salt.
10. Stir well and serve hot.

NUTRITIONS: Calories: 214 Cal Fat: 16.5 g Carbohydrates: 7.3 g Sugar: 3 g Protein: 11.6 g Cholesterol: 40 mg

CRACKPOT CHICKEN TACO SOUP

INGREDIENTS

- 2 frozen boneless chicken breast
- 2 cans of white beans or black beans
- 1 can of diced tomatoes
- Green chili's
- 1/2 onion chopped
- 1/2 packet of taco seasoning
- 1/2 teaspoon of Garlic salt
- 1 cup of chicken broth
- Salt and pepper to taste
- Tortilla chips, cheese sour cream and cilantro as toppings, as well as chili pepper (this is optional).

DIRECTIONS

1. Put your frozen chicken into the crock pot and place the other ingredients into the pool too.
2. Leave to cook for about 6-8 hours.
3. After cooking, take out the chicken and shred to the size you want.
4. Finally, place the shredded chicken into the crockpot and put it on a slow cooker. Stir and allow to cook.
5. You can add more beans and tomatoes also to help stretch the meat and make it tastier.

NUTRITIONS: Carbohydrates: 47 g Protein: 29 g Fat: 4 g Cholesterol: 48 mg Sodium: 1071 mg Fiber: 12 g

TOFU STIR FRY WITH ASPARAGUS

INGREDIENTS

- 1 pound asparagus, cut off stems
- 2 tbsp olive oil
- 2 blocks tofu, pressed and cubed
- 2 garlic cloves, minced
- 1 tsp. cajun spice mix
- 1 tsp. mustard
- 1 bell pepper, chopped
- 1/4 cup vegetable broth
- Salt and black pepper, to taste

DIRECTIONS

1. In a large saucepan with lightly salted water, place in asparagus and cook until tender for 10 minutes; drain.
2. Set a wok over high heat and warm olive oil; stir in tofu cubes and cook for 6 minutes.
3. Place in garlic and cook for 30 seconds until soft.
4. Stir in the rest of the ingredients, including reserved asparagus, and cook for an additional 4 minutes.
5. Divide among plates and serve.

NUTRITIONS: Calories: 138 Cal Fat: 8.9 g Carbohydrates: 5.9 g Protein: 6.4 g

CREAM OF THYME TOMATO SOUP

INGREDIENTS

- 2 tbsp ghee
- 2 large red onions, diced
- 1/2 cup raw cashew nuts, diced
- 2 (28 oz.) cans tomatoes
- 1 tsp. fresh thyme leaves + extra to garnish
- 1 1/2 cups water
- Salt and black pepper to taste

DIRECTIONS

1. Melt ghee in a pot over medium heat and sauté the onions for 4 minutes until softened.
2. Stir in the tomatoes, thyme, water, cashews, and season with salt and black pepper.
3. Cover and bring to simmer for 10 minutes until thoroughly cooked.
4. Open, turn the heat off, and puree the ingredients with an immersion blender.
5. Adjust to taste and stir in the heavy cream.
6. Spoon into soup bowls and serve.

NUTRITIONS: Calories: 310 Cal Fats: 27 g Carbohydrates: 3g Protein: 11g

MUSHROOM & JALAPEÑO STEW

INGREDIENTS

- 2 tsp. olive oil
- 1 cup leeks, chopped
- 1 garlic clove, minced
- 1/2 cup celery stalks, chopped
- 1/2 cup carrots, chopped
- 1 green bell pepper, chopped
- 1 jalapeño pepper, chopped
- 2 1/2 cups mushrooms, sliced
- 1 1/2 cups vegetable stock
- 2 tomatoes, chopped
- 2 thyme sprigs, chopped
- 1 rosemary sprig, chopped
- 2 bay leaves
- 1/2 tsp. salt
- 1/4 tsp. ground black pepper
- 2 tbsp vinegar

DIRECTIONS

1. Set a pot over medium heat and warm oil.
2. Add in garlic and leeks and sauté until soft and translucent.
3. Add in the black pepper, celery, mushrooms, and carrots.
4. Cook as you stir for 12 minutes; stir in a splash of vegetable stock to ensure there is no sticking.
5. Stir in the rest of the ingredients.
6. Set heat to medium; allow to simmer for 25 to 35 minutes or until cooked through.
7. Divide into individual bowls and serve warm.

NUTRITIONS: Calories: 65 Cal Fats: 2.7 g Carbohydrates: 9 g Protein: 2.7 g

EASY CAULIFLOWER SOUP

INGREDIENTS

- 2 tbsp olive oil
- 2 onions, finely chopped
- 1 tsp. garlic, minced
- 1 pound cauliflower, cut into florets
- 1 cup kale, chopped
- 4 cups vegetable broth
- 1/2 cup almond milk
- 1/2 tsp. salt
- 1/2 tsp. red pepper flakes
- 1 tbsp fresh chopped parsley

DIRECTIONS

1. Set a pot over medium heat and warm the oil.
2. Add garlic and onions and sauté until browned and softened.
3. Place in vegetable broth, kale, and cauliflower; cook for 10 minutes until the mixture boils.
4. Stir in the pepper flakes, salt, and almond milk; reduce the heat and simmer the soup for 5 minutes.
5. Transfer the soup to an immersion blender and blend to achieve the desired consistency; top with parsley and serve immediately.

NUTRITIONS: Calories: 172 Cal Fats: 10.3 g Carbohydrates: 11.8g Protein: 8.1 g

CAULIFLOWER SOUP

INGREDIENTS

- 2 cup cauliflower florets, diced
- 1 cup heavy cream
- 2 cup vegetable stock
- 1 tbsp chives, minced
- Salt and pepper to taste
- 1 garlic cloves, minced
- 1 tbsp almond butter

DIRECTIONS

1. In a large saucepan, add the almond butter.
2. Toss the garlic until it turns golden.
3. Add the cauliflower and toss for 2 minutes.
4. Add the vegetable stock and cook on high heat for 10 minutes.
5. Add the heavy cream, chives, salt, pepper, and cook for 8 minutes.
6. Serve hot.

NUTRITIONS: Fat: 5.5 g Cholesterol: 4.6 mg Sodium: 408 mg Potassium: 418 mg Carbohydrates: 16 g

LIME-MINT SOUP

INGREDIENTS

- 4 cups vegetable broth
- 1/4 cup fresh mint leaves, roughly chopped
- 1/4 cup chopped scallions, white and green parts
- 3 garlic cloves, minced
- 3 tablespoons freshly squeezed lime juice

DIRECTIONS

1. In a large stockpot, combine the broth, mint, scallions, garlic, and lime juice.
2. Bring to a boil over medium-high heat.
3. Cover, reduce the heat to low, simmer for 15 minutes, and serve.

NUTRITIONS: Fat: 2 g Carbohydrates: 5 g Fiber: 1 g Protein: 5 g

SAVORY SPLIT PEA SOUP

INGREDIENTS

- 1 (16-ounce) package dried green split peas, soaked overnight
- 5 cups vegetable broth or water
- 2 teaspoons garlic powder
- 2 teaspoons onion powder
- 1 teaspoon dried oregano
- 1 teaspoon dried thyme
- 1/4 teaspoon freshly ground black pepper

DIRECTIONS

1. In a large stockpot, combine the split peas, broth, garlic powder, onion powder, oregano, thyme, and pepper.
2. Bring to a boil over medium-high heat.
3. Cover, reduce the heat to medium-low, and simmer for 45 minutes, stirring every 5 to 10 minutes. Serve warm.

NUTRITIONS: Fat: 2 g Carbohydrates: 48 g Fiber: 20 g Protein: 23 g

CHAPTER 21. SMOOTHIES

AVOCADO BLUEBERRY SMOOTHIE

INGREDIENTS

- 1 tsp chia seeds
- ½ cup unsweetened coconut milk
- 1 avocado
- ½ cup blueberries

DIRECTIONS

1. Add all the listed ingredients to the blender and blend until smooth and creamy.
2. Serve immediately and enjoy.

NUTRITIONS: Calories: 389 Fat: 34.6g Carbs: 20.7g   Protein: 4.8g Fiber: 0g

VEGAN BLUEBERRY SMOOTHIE

INGREDIENTS

- 2 cups blueberries
- 1 tbsp hemp seeds
- 1 tbsp chia seeds
- 1 tbsp flax meal
- 1/8 tsp orange zest, grated
- 1 cup fresh orange juice
- 1 cup unsweetened coconut milk

DIRECTIONS

1. Toss all your ingredients into your blender then process till smooth and creamy.
2. Serve immediately and enjoy.

NUTRITIONS: Calories: 212 Fat: 6.6g Carbs: 36.9g Protein: 5.2g Fiber: 0g

BERRY PEACH SMOOTHIE

INGREDIENTS

- » 1 cup coconut water
- » 1 tbsp hemp seeds
- » 1 tbsp agave
- » ½ cup strawberries
- » ½ cup blueberries
- » ½ cup cherries
- » ½ cup peaches

DIRECTIONS

1. Toss all your ingredients into your blender then process till smooth and creamy.
2. Serve immediately and enjoy.

NUTRITIONS: Calories: 117 Fat: 2.5g Carbs: 22.5g Protein: 3.5g Fiber: 0g

CANTALOUPE BLACKBERRY SMOOTHIE

INGREDIENTS

- » 1 cup coconut milk yogurt
- » ½ cup blackberries
- » 2 cups fresh cantaloupe
- » 1 banana

DIRECTIONS

1. Toss all your ingredients into your blender then process till smooth.
2. Serve and enjoy.

NUTRITIONS: Calories: 160 Fat: 4.5g Carbs: 33.7g Protein: 1.8g Fiber: 0g

CANTALOUPE KALE SMOOTHIE

INGREDIENTS

- 8 oz. water
- 1 orange, peeled
- 3 cups kale, chopped
- 1 banana, peeled
- 2 cups cantaloupe, chopped
- 1 zucchini, chopped

DIRECTIONS

1. Toss all your ingredients into your blender then process till smooth and creamy.
2. Serve immediately and enjoy.

NUTRITIONS: Calories: 203 Fat: 0.5g Carbs: 49.2g Protein: 5.6g Fiber: 0g

MIX BERRY CANTALOUPE SMOOTHIE

INGREDIENTS

- 1 cup alkaline water
- 2 fresh Seville orange juices
- ¼ cup fresh mint leaves
- 1 ½ cups mixed berries
- 2 cups cantaloupe

DIRECTIONS

1. Toss all your ingredients into your blender then process till smooth.
2. Serve immediately and enjoy.

NUTRITIONS: Calories: 122 Fat: 1g Carbs: 26.1g Protein: 2.4g Fiber: 0g

AVOCADO KALE SMOOTHIE

INGREDIENTS

- 1 cup water
- ½ Seville orange, peeled
- 1 avocado
- 1 cucumber, peeled
- 1 cup kale
- 1 cup ice cubes

DIRECTIONS

1. Toss all your ingredients into your blender then process till smooth and creamy.
2. Serve immediately and enjoy.

NUTRITIONS: Calories: 160 Fat: 13.3g Carbs: 11.6g Protein: 2.4g Fiber: 0g

APPLE KALE CUCUMBER SMOOTHIE

INGREDIENTS

- ¾ cup water
- ½ green apple, diced
- ¾ cup kale
- ½ cucumber

DIRECTIONS

1. Toss all your ingredients into your blender then process till smooth and creamy.
2. Serve immediately and enjoy.

NUTRITIONS: Calories: 86 Fat: 0.5g Carbs: 21.7g Protein: 1.9g Fiber: 0g

REFRESHING CUCUMBER SMOOTHIE

INGREDIENTS

- 1 cup ice cubes
- 20 drops liquid stevia
- 2 fresh lime, peeled and halved
- 1 tsp lime zest, grated
- 1 cucumber, chopped
- 1 avocado, pitted and peeled
- 2 cups kale
- 1 tbsp creamed coconut
- ¾ cup coconut water

DIRECTIONS

1. Toss all your ingredients into your blender then process till smooth and creamy.
2. Serve immediately and enjoy.

NUTRITIONS: Calories: 313 Fat: 25.1g Carbs: 24.7g Protein: 4.9g Fiber: 0g

CAULIFLOWER VEGGIE SMOOTHIE

INGREDIENTS

- 1 zucchini, peeled and chopped
- 1 Seville orange, peeled
- 1 apple, diced
- 1 banana
- 1 cup kale
- ½ cup cauliflower

DIRECTIONS

1. Toss all your ingredients into your blender then process till smooth and creamy.
2. Serve immediately and enjoy.

NUTRITIONS: Calories: 71 Fat: 0.3g Carbs: 18.3g Protein: 1.3g Fiber: 0g

SOURSOP SMOOTHIE

INGREDIENTS

- 3 quartered frozen Burro Bananas
- 1-1/2 cups of Homemade Coconut Milk
- 1/4 cup of Walnuts
- 1 teaspoon of Sea Moss Gel
- 1 teaspoon of Ground Ginger
- 1 teaspoon of Soursop Leaf Powder
- 1 handful of Kale

DIRECTIONS

1. Prepare and put all ingredients in a blender or a food processor.
2. Blend it well until you reach a smooth consistency.
3. Serve and enjoy your Soursop Smoothie!
4. Useful Tips:
5. If you don't have frozen Bananas, you can use fresh ones.

NUTRITIONS: Calories: 213 Fat: 3.1g Carbs: 6g Protein: 8g Fiber: 4.3g

CUCUMBER-GINGER WATER

INGREDIENTS

- 1 sliced Cucumber
- 1 smashed thumb of Ginger Root
- 2 cups of Spring Water

DIRECTIONS

1. Prepare and put all ingredients in a jar with a lid.
2. Let the water infuse overnight. Store it in the refrigerator.
3. Serve and enjoy your Cucumber-Ginger Water throughout the day!

NUTRITIONS: Calories: 117 Fat: 2g Carbs: 6g Protein: 9.7g Fiber: 2g

STRAWBERRY MILKSHAKE

INGREDIENTS

- 2 cups of Homemade Hempseed Milk
- 1 cup of frozen Strawberries
- Agave Syrup, to taste

DIRECTIONS

1. Prepare and put all ingredients in a blender or a food processor.
2. Blend it well until you reach a smooth consistency.
3. Serve and enjoy your Strawberry Milkshake!
4. Useful Tips
5. If you don't have Homemade Hempseed Milk, you can add Homemade Walnut Milk instead.
6. If you don't have frozen Strawberries, you can use fresh ones.

NUTRITIONS: Calories: 222 Fat: 4g Carbs: 3g Protein: 6g Fiber: 1g

CACTUS SMOOTHIE

INGREDIENTS

- 1 medium Cactus
- 2 cups of Homemade Coconut Milk
- 2 frozen Baby Bananas
- 1/2 cup of Walnuts
- 1 Date
- 2 teaspoons of Hemp Seeds

DIRECTIONS

1. Take the Cactus, remove all pricks, wash it, and cut into medium pieces.
2. Put all the listed ingredients in a blender or a food processor.
3. Blend it well until you reach a smooth consistency.
4. Serve and enjoy your Cactus Smoothie!
5. Useful Tips
6. If you don't have Homemade Coconut Milk, you can add Homemade Walnut Milk or Homemade Hempseed Milk instead.
7. If you don't have frozen Bananas, you can use fresh ones.
8. If you don't have Baby Bananas, add 1 Burro Banana instead.

NUTRITIONS: Calories: 123 Fat: 3g Carbs: 6g Protein: 2.5g Fiber: 0g

PRICKLY PEAR JUICE

INGREDIENTS

- 6 Prickly Pears
- 1/3 cup of Lime Juice
- 1/3 cup of Agave
- 1-1/2 cups of Spring Water*

DIRECTIONS

1. Take Prickly Pear, cut off the ends, slice off the skin, and put in a blender. Do the same with the other pears.
2. Add Lime Juice with Agave to the blender and blend well for 30–40 seconds.
3. Strain the prepared mixture through a nut milk bag or cheesecloth and pour it back into the blender.
4. Pour Spring Water in and blend it repeatedly.
5. Serve and enjoy your Prickly Pear Juice!
6. Useful Tips:
7. If you want a cold drink, add a tray of ice cubes instead.
8. like and serve it on top of the braised greens.

NUTRITIONS: Calories: 312 Fat: 6g Carbs: 11g Protein: 8g Fiber: 2g

CUCUMBER-GINGER WATER

INGREDIENTS

- 1 sliced Cucumber
- 1 smashed thumb of Ginger Root
- 2 cups of Spring Water

DIRECTIONS

1. Prepare and put all ingredients in a jar with a lid.
2. Let the water infuse overnight. Store it in the refrigerator.
3. Serve and enjoy your Cucumber-Ginger Water throughout the day!

NUTRITIONS: Calories: 117 Fat: 2g Carbs: 6g Protein: 9.7g Fiber: 2g

CHAPTER 22.
DESSERTS

ASPARAGUS GREEN SCRAMBLE

INGREDIENTS

- 3 eggs
- 1 Portobello mushroom, chopped
- 2 garlic cloves, chopped
- 1/2 cup spinach
- 4 asparagus, trimmed, diced
- Sea salt to taste
- Cayenne pepper to taste
- 1 tbsp olive oil

DIRECTIONS

1. In a bowl, whisk the eggs with salt and cayenne pepper.
2. In a skillet, add the oil and pour in the egg mix.
3. Cook for 1 minute.
4. Add the spinach, mushroom, asparagus, and garlic.
5. Stir for 4 minutes. Serve.

NUTRITIONS: Carbohydrates: 3 g Fat: 6 g Protein: 13 g

NO BAKE FUELING PEANUT BUTTER BROWNIES

COOKING: 30'   **PREPARATION: 5'**   **SERVES: 6**

INGREDIENTS

- 3 tablespoons peanut butter
- 1 cup water
- 6 packets Double Chocolate Brownie Fueling

DIRECTIONS

1. Put all ingredients in a bowl and mix until all elements are well incorporated.
2. Pour into silicone molds and place in the freezer.
3. Freeze for 30 minutes before eating.

NUTRITIONS: Calories per serving: 906 Cal Protein: 8.7 g Carbohydrates: 157 g Fat: 31.8 g Sugar: 1.5 g

PEANUT BUTTER BROWNIE ICE CREAM SANDWICHES

INGREDIENTS

- 1 packet Medifast Brownie Mix
- 3 tablespoons water
- 1 Peanut Butter Crunch Bar or any bar of your choice
- 2 tablespoons Peanut Butter Powder
- 1 tablespoon water
- 2 tablespoons cool whip

DIRECTIONS

1. Melt the Brownie Mix with water.
2. Add in the Peanut Butter Crunch until a dough is formed.
3. Spoon 4 dough balls on a plate and flatten using the palm of your hands.
4. Make sure that the dough is 1/4 inch thick.
5. Place in a microwave oven and cook for 2 minutes.
6. Meanwhile, mix the Peanut Butter Powder and water to form a paste.
7. Add cool whip. Set aside in the fridge to chill for at least 1 hour.
8. Take the cookies out from the microwave oven and allow to cool.
9. Once cooled, spoon the Peanut Butter ice cream in between two cookies.
10. Serve immediately.

NUTRITIONS: Calories per serving: 410 Cal Protein: 8.3 g Carbohydrates: 57.6 g Fat: 13.2 g Sugar: 5.3g

CRANBERRY SALAD

INGREDIENTS

- 1 Sugar free cranberry jello pack (1/2 cup for snacks allowed)
- 1/2 cup celery chopped (1 green)
- 7 Half Cut Walnut (1 snack)

DIRECTIONS

1. Jello mix according to the instructions of the box.
2. Attach walnuts and celery.
3. Allow setting.
4. Shake until serving.
5. Requires servings in 4-1/2 cups.

NUTRITIONS: Fats: 11 g Sodium: 73 mg Potassium: 212 mg Carbohydrates: 54 g Protein: 4.1 g

RECIPES COOKBOOK FOR BEGINNERS

CHICKEN SALAD WITH PINEAPPLE AND PECANS

INGREDIENTS

- (6-ounce) Boneless, skinless, cooked and cubed chicken breast
- Tablespoons of celery hacked
- Cut 1/4 cup of pineapple
- 1/4 cup orange peeled segments
- Tablespoon of pecans hacked
- 1/4 cup seedless grapes
- Salt and black chili pepper, to taste
- Cups cut from roman lettuce

DIRECTIONS

1. Put chicken, celery, pineapple, grapes, pecans, and raisins in a medium dish.
2. Kindly blend until mixed with a spoon, then season with salt and pepper.
3. Create a bed of lettuce on a plate.
4. Cover with mixture of chicken and serve.

NUTRITIONS: Calories: 386 Cal Carbohydrates: 20 g Fat: 19 g Protein: 25 g

ZUCCHINI FRITTER

INGREDIENTS

- 1 1/2 pound of grated zucchini
- 1 Tsp. of salt
- 1/4 cup of grated Parmesan
- 1/4 cup of flour
- 2 cloves of minced garlic
- 2 Tbsp of olive oil
- 1 large egg
- Freshly ground black pepper and kosher salt to taste

DIRECTIONS

1. Put the grated zucchini into a colander over the sink
2. Add your salt and toss it to mix properly, then leave it to settle for about 10 minutes.
3. Next, use a clean cheese cloth to drain the zucchini completely.
4. Combine drained zucchini, Parmesan, garlic, flour, and the beaten egg in a large bowl, mix, and season with pepper and salt.
5. Next, heat the olive oil in a skillet applying medium-high heat.
6. Use a tablespoon to scoop batter for each cake, put in the oil, and flatten using a spatula.
7. Allow to cook until the underside is richly golden brown, then flip over to the other side and cook.
8. Your delicious Zucchini fritters are ready to be served.

NUTRITIONS: Total Fat: 12.0 g Cholesterol: 101.9 mg Sodium: 728.9 mg Total Carbohydrate: 11.9 g Dietary Fiber: 1.9 g Sugars: 4.6 g Protein: 8.6 g

HEALTHY BROCCOLI SALAD

INGREDIENTS

- 3 cups broccoli, chopped
- 1 tbsp apple cider vinegar
- 1/2 cup Greek yogurt
- 2 tbsp sunflower seeds
- 3 bacon slices, cooked and chopped
- 1/3 cup onion, sliced
- 1/4 tsp. stevia

DIRECTIONS

1. In a mixing bowl, mix broccoli, onion, and bacon.
2. In a small bowl, mix yogurt, vinegar, and stevia and pour over broccoli mixture.
3. Stir to combine.
4. Sprinkle sunflower seeds on top of the salad.
5. Store salad in the refrigerator for 30 minutes.
6. Serve and enjoy.

NUTRITIONS: Calories: 90 Cal Fat: 4.9 g Carbohydrates: 5.4 g Sugar: 2.5 g Protein: 6.2 g Cholesterol: 12 mg

BISCUIT PIZZA

INGREDIENTS

- 1 sachet Buttermilk Cheddar and Herb Biscuit
- 2 tablespoons water
- 1 tablespoon tomato sauce
- 1 tablespoon low fat cheese, shredded

DIRECTIONS

1. Preheat the oven or toaster to 3500F for 5 minutes.
2. In a bowl, stir the Buttermilk Cheddar and Herb Biscuit with water to form a thick paste. Spread into a thin circle on a baking tray lined with parch- ment paper.
3. Cook for 10 minutes to harden.
4. Once harden, spread tomato sauce on top and cheese.
5. Bake for another 5 minutes.

NUTRITIONS: Calories per serving: 437 Cal Protein: 9.5 g Carbohydrates: 68.5 g Fat: 5.3 g Sugar: 4.3 g

GRANOLA

INGREDIENTS

- 1 package Oatmeal
- 1 packet stevia
- 1 teaspoon vanilla extract
- 1/2 teaspoon apple spice or pumpkin pie spice

DIRECTIONS

1. Preheat the oven to 400oF. In a bowl, combine all ingredients and add enough water to get the granola to stick together.
2. Drop the granola onto a cookie sheet lined with parchment paper.
3. Bake for 8 minutes but make sure to give the granola a fair shake for even browning halfway through the cooking time.

NUTRITIONS: Calories per serving: 209 Cal Protein: 5.8 g Carbohydrates: 42 g Fat: 3.2 g Sugar: 6.2 g

DELICIOUS ZUCCHINI QUICHE

INGREDIENTS

- 6 eggs
- 2 medium zucchini, shredded
- 1/2 tsp. dried basil
- 2 garlic cloves, minced
- 1 tbsp dry onion, minced
- 2 tbsp parmesan cheese, grated
- 2 tbsp fresh parsley, chopped
- 1/2 cup olive oil
- 1 cup cheddar cheese, shredded
- 1/4 cup coconut flour
- 3/4 cup almond flour
- 1/2 tsp. salt

DIRECTIONS

1. Preheat the oven to 350 F.
2. Grease 9-inch pie dish and set aside.
3. Squeeze out excess liquid from zucchini.
4. Add all ingredients into the large bowl and mix until well combined.
5. Pour into the prepared pie dish.
6. Bake in preheated oven for 45-60 minutes or until set.
7. Remove from the oven and let it cool completely.
8. Slice and serve.

NUTRITIONS: Calories: 288 Cal Fat: 26.3 g Carbohydrates: 5 g Sugar: 1.6 g Protein: 11 g Cholesterol: 139 mg

COBB SALAD WITH BLUE CHEESE DRESSING

INGREDIENTS

- Dressing:
- 1/2 cup buttermilk
- 1 cup mayonnaise
- 2 tbsp Worcestershire sauce
- 1/2 cup sour cream
- 1 1/2 cup crumbled blue cheese
- Salt and black pepper to taste
- 2 tbsp chopped chives
- Salad:
- 6 eggs
- 2 chicken breasts, boneless and skinless
- 5 strips bacon
- 1 iceberg lettuce, cut into chunks
- 1 romaine lettuce, chopped
- 1 bibb lettuce, cored and leaves removed
- 2 avocado, pitted and diced
- 2 large tomatoes, chopped
- 1/2 cup crumbled blue cheese
- 2 scallions, chopped

DIRECTIONS

1. In a bowl, whisk the buttermilk, mayonnaise, Worcestershire sauce, and sour cream.
2. Stir in the blue cheese, salt, black pepper, and chives. Place in the refrigerator to chill until ready to use.
3. Bring the eggs to boil in salted water over medium heat for 10 minutes.
4. Once ready, drain the eggs and transfer to the ice bath. Peel and chop the eggs. Set aside.
5. Preheat the grill pan over high heat. Season the chicken with salt and pepper.
6. Grill for 3 minutes on each side. Remove to a plate to cool for 3 minutes, and cut into bite-size chunks.
7. Fry the bacon in another pan set over medium heat until crispy, about 6 minutes. Remove, let cool for 2 minutes, and chop.
8. Arrange the lettuce leaves in a salad bowl and add the avocado, tomatoes, eggs, bacon, and chicken in single piles.
9. Sprinkle the blue cheese over the salad as well as the scallions and black pepper.
10. Drizzle the blue cheese dressing on the salad and serve with low carb bread.

NUTRITIONS: Calories: 122 Cal Fats: 14 g Carbohydrates: 2 g Protein: 23 g

VANILLA BEAN FRAPPUCCINO

INGREDIENTS

- 3 cups unsweetened vanilla almond milk, chilled
- 2 tsp. swerve
- 1 1/2 cups heavy cream, cold
- 1 vanilla bean
- 1/4 tsp. xanthan gum
- Unsweetened chocolate shavings to garnish

DIRECTIONS

1. Combine the almond milk, swerve, heavy cream, vanilla bean, and xanthan gum in the blender, and process on high speed for 1 minute until smooth. \
2. Pour into tall shake glasses, sprinkle with chocolate shavings, and serve immediately.

NUTRITIONS: Calories: 193 Cal Fats: 14 g Carbohydrates: 6 g Protein: 15 g

DARK CHOCOLATE MOCHACCINO ICE BOMBS

INGREDIENTS

- 1/2 pound cream cheese
- 4 tbsp powdered sweetener
- 2 ounces strong coffee
- 2 tbsp cocoa powder, unsweetened
- 1 ounce cocoa butter, melted
- 2 1/2 ounces dark chocolate, melted

DIRECTIONS

1. Combine cream cheese, sweetener, coffee, and cocoa powder, in a food processor.
2. Roll 2 tbsp of the mixture and place on a lined tray.
3. Mix the melted cocoa butter and chocolate, and coat the bombs with it.
4. Freeze for 2 hours.

NUTRITIONS: Calories: 127 Cal Fats: 13g Carbohydrates: 1.4 g Protein: 1.9 g

CHOCOLATE BARK WITH ALMONDS

INGREDIENTS

- 1/2 cup toasted almonds, chopped
- 1/2 cup butter
- 10 drops stevia
- 1/4 tsp. salt
- 1/2 cup unsweetened coconut flakes
- 4 ounces dark chocolate

DIRECTIONS

1. Melt together the butter and chocolate, in the microwave, for 90 seconds.
2. Remove and stir in stevia.
3. Line a cookie sheet with waxed paper and spread the chocolate evenly.
4. Scatter the almonds on top, coconut flakes, and sprinkle with salt.
5. Refrigerate for one hour.

NUTRITIONS: Calories: 161 Cal Fats: 15.3 g Carbohydrates: 1.9 g Protein: 1.9 g

CHAPTER 23.
DESSERTS

CHOCOLATE BARS

INGREDIENTS

- 15 oz cream cheese, softened
- 15 oz unsweetened dark chocolate
- 1 tsp vanilla
- 10 drops liquid stevia

DIRECTIONS

1. Grease 8-inch square dish and set aside.
2. In a saucepan dissolve chocolate over low heat.
3. Add stevia and vanilla and stir well.
4. Remove pan from heat and set aside.
5. Add cream cheese into the blender and blend until smooth.
6. Add melted chocolate mixture into the cream cheese and blend until just combined.
7. Transfer mixture into the prepared dish and spread evenly and place in the refrigerator until firm.
8. Slice and serve.

NUTRITIONS: Calories: 230 Fat: 24 g Carbs: 7.5 g Sugar: 0.1 g Protein: 6 g Cholesterol: 29 mg

BLUEBERRY MUFFINS

INGREDIENTS

- 2 eggs
- 1/2 cup fresh blueberries
- 1 cup heavy cream
- 2 cups almond flour
- 1/4 tsp lemon zest
- 1/2 tsp lemon extract
- 1 tsp baking powder
- 5 drops stevia
- 1/4 cup butter, melted

DIRECTIONS

1. heat the cooker to 350 F. Line muffin tin with cupcake liners and set aside.
2. Add eggs into the bowl and whisk until mix.
3. Add remaining ingredients and mix to combine.
4. Pour mixture into the prepared muffin tin and bake for 25 minutes.
5. Serve and enjoy.

NUTRITIONS: Calories: 190 Fat: 17 g Carbs: 5 g Sugar: 1 g Protein: 5 g Cholesterol: 55 mg

CHIA PUDDING

INGREDIENTS

- 4 tbsp chia seeds
- 1 cup unsweetened coconut milk
- 1/2 cup raspberries

DIRECTIONS

1. Add raspberry and coconut milk into a blender and blend until smooth.
2. Pour mixture into the glass jar.
3. Add chia seeds in a jar and stir well.
4. Seal the jar with a lid and shake well and place in the refrigerator for 3 hours.
5. Serve chilled and enjoy.

NUTRITIONS: Calories: 360 Fat: 33 g Carbs: 13 g Sugar: 5 g Protein: 6 g Cholesterol: 0 mg

AVOCADO PUDDING

INGREDIENTS

- 2 ripe avocados, pitted and cut into pieces
- 1 tbsp fresh lime juice
- 14 oz can coconut milk
- 2 tsp liquid stevia
- 2 tsp vanilla

DIRECTIONS

1. Inside the blender Add all ingredients and blend until smooth.
2. Serve immediately and enjoy.

NUTRITIONS: Calories: 317 Fat: 30 g Carbs: 9 g Sugar: 0.5 g Protein: 3 g Cholesterol: 0 mg

DELICIOUS BROWNIE BITES

INGREDIENTS

- 1/4 cup unsweetened chocolate chips
- 1/4 cup unsweetened cocoa powder
- 1 cup pecans, chopped
- 1/2 cup almond butter
- 1/2 tsp vanilla
- 1/4 cup monk fruit sweetener
- 1/8 tsp pink salt

DIRECTIONS

1. Add pecans, sweetener, vanilla, almond butter, cocoa powder, and salt into the food processor and process until well combined.
2. Transfer brownie mixture into the large bowl. Add chocolate chips and fold well.
3. Make small round shape balls from brownie mixture and place onto a baking tray.
4. Place in the freezer for 20 minutes.
5. Serve and enjoy.

NUTRITIONS: Calories: 108 Fat: 9 g Carbs: 4 g Sugar: 1 g Protein: 2 g Cholesterol: 0 mg

PUMPKIN BALLS

INGREDIENTS

- 1 cup almond butter
- 5 drops liquid stevia
- 2 tbsp coconut flour
- 2 tbsp pumpkin puree
- 1 tsp pumpkin pie spice

DIRECTIONS

1. Mix together pumpkin puree in a large bowl, and almond butter until well combined.
2. Add liquid stevia, pumpkin pie spice, and coconut flour and mix well.
3. Make small balls from mixture and place onto a baking tray.
4. Place in the freezer for 1 hour.
5. Serve and enjoy.

NUTRITIONS: Calories: 96 Fat: 8 g Carbs: 4 g Sugar: 1 g Protein: 2 g Cholesterol: 0 mg

SMOOTH PEANUT BUTTER CREAM

INGREDIENTS

- 1/4 cup peanut butter
- 4 overripe bananas, chopped
- 1/3 cup cocoa powder
- 1/4 tsp vanilla extract
- 1/8 tsp salt

DIRECTIONS

1. In the blender add all the listed ingredients and blend until smooth.
2. Serve immediately and enjoy.

NUTRITIONS: Calories: 101 Fat: 5 g Carbs: 14 g Sugar: 7 g Protein: 3 g Cholesterol: 0 mg

VANILLA AVOCADO POPSICLES

INGREDIENTS

- 2 avocadoes
- 1 tsp vanilla
- 1 cup almond milk
- 1 tsp liquid stevia
- 1/2 cup unsweetened cocoa powder

DIRECTIONS

1. In the blender add all the listed ingredients and blend smoothly.
2. Pour blended mixture into the Popsicle molds and place in the freezer until set.
3. Serve and enjoy.

NUTRITIONS: Calories: 130 Fat: 12 g Carbs: 7 g Sugar: 1 g Protein: 3 g Cholesterol: 0 mg

CHOCOLATE POPSICLE

INGREDIENTS

- 4 oz unsweetened chocolate, chopped
- 6 drops liquid stevia
- 1 1/2 cups heavy cream

DIRECTIONS

1. Add heavy cream into the microwave-safe bowl and microwave until just begins the boiling.
2. Add chocolate into the heavy cream and set aside for 5 minutes.
3. Add liquid stevia into the heavy cream mixture and stir until chocolate is melted.
4. Pour mixture into the Popsicle molds and place in freezer for 4 hours or until set.
5. Serve and enjoy.

NUTRITIONS: Calories: 198 Fat: 21 g Carbs: 6 g Sugar: 0.2 g Protein: 3 g Cholesterol: 41 mg

RASPBERRY ICE CREAM

INGREDIENTS

- 1 cup frozen raspberries
- 1/2 cup heavy cream
- 1/8 tsp stevia powder

DIRECTIONS

1. Blend all the listed ingredients in a blender until smooth.
2. Serve immediately and enjoy.

NUTRITIONS: Calories: 144 Fat: 11 g Carbs: 10 g Sugar: 4 g Protein: 2 g Cholesterol: 41 mg

CHOCOLATE FROSTY

INGREDIENTS

- 2 tbsp unsweetened cocoa powder
- 1 cup heavy whipping cream
- 1 tbsp almond butter
- 5 drops liquid stevia
- 1 tsp vanilla

DIRECTIONS

1. Add cream into the medium bowl and beat using the hand mixer for 5 minutes.
2. Add remaining ingredients and blend until thick cream form.
3. Pour in serving bowls and place them in the freezer for 30 minutes.
4. Serve and enjoy.

NUTRITIONS: Calories: 137 Fat: 13 g Carbs: 3 g Sugar: 0.5 g Protein: 2 g Cholesterol: 41 mg

CHOCOLATE ALMOND BUTTER BROWNIE

INGREDIENTS

- 1 cup bananas, overripe
- 1/2 cup almond butter, melted
- 1 scoop protein powder
- 2 tbsp unsweetened cocoa powder

DIRECTIONS

1. Preheat the air fryer to 325 F. Grease air fryer baking pan and set aside.
2. Blend all ingredients in a blender until smooth.
3. Pour batter into the prepared pan and place in the air fryer basket and cook for 16 minutes.
4. Serve and enjoy.

NUTRITIONS: Calories: 82 Fat: 2 g Carbs: 11 g Sugar: 5 g Protein: 7 g Cholesterol: 16 mg

PEANUT BUTTER FUDGE

INGREDIENTS

- 1/4 cup almonds, toasted and chopped
- 12 oz smooth peanut butter
- 15 drops liquid stevia
- 3 tbsp coconut oil
- 4 tbsp coconut cream
- Pinch of salt

DIRECTIONS

1. Line baking tray with parchment paper.
2. Melt coconut oil in a pan over low heat. Add peanut butter, coconut cream, stevia, and salt in a saucepan. Stir well.
3. Pour fudge mixture into the prepared baking tray and sprinkle chopped almonds on top.
4. Place the tray in the refrigerator for 1 hour or until set.
5. Slice and serve.

NUTRITIONS: Calories: 131 Fat: 12 g Carbs: 4 g Sugar: 2 g Protein: 5 g Cholesterol: 0 mg

ALMOND BUTTER FUDGE

INGREDIENTS

- 3/4 cup creamy almond butter
- 1 1/2 cups unsweetened chocolate chips

DIRECTIONS

1. Line 8*4-inch pan with parchment paper and set aside.
2. Add chocolate chips and almond butter into the double boiler and cook over medium heat until the chocolate-butter mixture is melted. Stir well.
3. place mixture into the prepared pan and place in the freezer until set.
4. Slice and serve.

NUTRITIONS: Calories: 197 Fat: 16 g Carbs: 7 g Sugar: 1 g Protein: 4 g Cholesterol: 0 mg

CONCLUSION

The 5&1 Diet has been subjected to various studies to prove its efficacy in weight loss. Different studies were published in various journals indicating that those who follow this program are able to see significant changes in as little as 8 weeks and that people can achieve their long-term health goals with the 5&1 Diet.

While the initial 5&1 ideal weight plan is quite restrictive, maintenance phases 3&3 allow for greater variety of less processed foods and snacks, which can facilitate weight loss.

Under this diet regimen, dieters are required to follow a weight plan that includes five fueling a day and one lean green meal daily. However, there are also other regimens of the 5&1 Diet if the five fuels a day is too much for you. And since this is a commercial diet, you have access to 5&1 coaches and become part of a community that will encourage you to succeed in your weight loss journey. Moreover, this diet is also designed for people who want to transition from their old habits to healthier ones.

The diet is a set of three programs, two of which focus on weight loss and one that is best for weight maintenance, if you are not trying to lose weight. The plans are high in protein and low in carbohydrates and calories to stimulate weight loss. Each program requires you to eat at least half of the food in the form of numerous 5&1 healthy prepackaged foods.

Since the plan requires the intake of carbohydrates, protein and fat, it is also a relatively balanced plan when it comes to food groups.

When it comes to weight loss, experts say that while 5&1 can help because it is essentially less caloric, it is unlikely to improve your eating habits permanently. You are more likely to gain weight after stopping the diet.

Also, diet experts warn that this pattern may not contain enough calories to meet your body's needs. "In terms of overall health and nutrition, as well as convenience, this diet isn't at the top of my list of best approaches." she says.

If you are interested in trying this, consider working with an experienced registered dietitian who can help you stay properly fed as you strive to achieve your desired weight.

For the most desirable 5 and 1 weight plan, eat 5 foods per day, plus a low carb lean meal and a low carb elective snack.

Although Initial Plan 5 & 1 is reasonably restrictive, Protection Segment 3 & 3 allows for a greater variety of less processed foods and snacks, which can also make weight loss easier and more persistent for long period

The bottom line is, that the 5&1 weight loss plan promotes weight loss via low calorie prepackaged meals; low carb homemade food, and personalized coaching; at the same time, as this system promotes quick-time period weight and fat loss, similarly research is wanted to assess whether it encourages the everlasting way of life adjustments needed for long-time period achievement.